ENDS AND MEANS OF REDUCING INCOME POVERTY

ROBERT J. LAMPMAN
University of Wisconsin

**Institute for Research on
Poverty Monograph Series**

MARKHAM PUBLISHING COMPANY/Chicago

INSTITUTE FOR RESEARCH ON POVERTY MONOGRAPH SERIES

This book is one of a Series sponsored by the Institute for Research on Poverty of the University of Wisconsin pursuant to the provisions of the Economic Opportunity Act of 1964.

This study was also supported in various ways by the Health Economics Research Center at the University of Wisconsin.

el

Printed in U.S.A.
Library of Congress Catalog Card Number 70-163340
Hardcover Standard Book Number 8410-0300-9
Paperback Standard Book Number 8410-0306-8

To my family

PREFACE

This book is about the origin and nature of the goal of reducing income poverty, the process by which that goal has been and is being accomplished, and the range of approaches open to us for continuing and accelerating that process. The mood of Part A is that of the social philosopher. Part B is an exercise in social accounting, or what Sir William Petty called "political arithmetick." Only in Part C does the mood shift, and only partially so, to what John R. Commons would have recognized as that of "social engineering." Throughout, the effort has been to avoid partisanship and to show the range of possibilities and to suggest the costs as well as the benefits of them. However, there are certain themes which are developed. These include the following:

1) The goal of reduction of income poverty is an important addition to the list of the nation's economic goals. It grows out of a long concern with inequality and debate over the consequences of policies to reduce inequality. The questions of how to set the poverty line and how fast to reduce income poverty remain, at bottom, matters for judgment.

2) It is useful to distinguish poverty from other aspects of inequality and further to separate "income poverty" from other types of poverty. Identifying income poverty as the problem predisposes one to favor remedies which increase incomes. It also heightens one's sensitivities to vertical and horizontal equities which are at issue in discussion of alternative means to reduce poverty. This heightened sensitivity is associated with what is called herein the "mentality" of the student of progressive income taxation.

3) The long record of income-poverty reduction can be understood by reference to several "strategies against poverty" which have been employed pragmatically throughout our colonial and national history. Further understanding of the record comes from study of demographic change, the mobility of the population in response to opportunities opened up by economic growth, and the workings of a public-private redistributional system which is strongly pro-poor in character. The tax-contribution system is only mildly redistributive toward the poor, but annual expenditures amounting to over $50 billion are now being made to the benefit of the poor. (That total, which includes a part of

such broad societal outlays as those on health and education, is a measure of the scope of the war on poverty.)

4) Successful poverty reduction from 1947 to 1967 gives a basis for hope that income poverty, as defined in 1964, can be eliminated in the current decade by continued pursuit of the strategies of facilitating the working of a market system, adapting the system to the needs of the poor, changing the poor to fit the system, and relieving the distress of the poor. More specifically, elimination of income poverty in a short period of time can best be expedited by concentrating our attention primarily on economic growth, employment and training opportunites for the poor, and cash transfers. With regard to the latter, attention should be devoted to the great majority of the poor who are not now eligible for such transfers (see the summary recommendations at pp. 153–68).

5) We should avoid understating efforts and progress that have been made to date on the reduction of income poverty. On the other hand, we should not forget that the poverty question (of which income poverty is one component) is only a part of larger social and economic and political questions, the priorities for which are difficult to establish. Moreover, although the record shows that social innovation can be successful, we need to appreciate the costs, including the forgoing of other achievements, associated with particular methods of poverty reduction.

This book was completed in 1970, six years after the beginning of the so-called war on poverty. In the six intervening years many books, articles, and speeches have been written on the many different aspects of poverty. This is not a treatise on that literature but simply another part of that great outpouring. As already indicated, this essay concentrates on only one of the social goals implicit in the Economic Opportunity Act, namely the reduction of income poverty. It is, in a way, a kind of summary of the author's writings on this subject over a twenty-year period (listed at pp. 169–71 as "Background Writings by the Author"). It draws heavily upon several of those writings. Part A is based in large part on "Recent Thought on Egalitarianism" (1957), "Ends and Means in the War on Poverty" (1966), "Income Distribution and Poverty" (1965), and "The Anti-Poverty Program in Historical Perspective" (1965). Part B is an extension of a paper on *The Low Income Population and Economic Growth,* published by the U.S. Congress Joint Economic Committee in 1959, and includes material first developed in "Population Growth and Poverty Reduction" (1966), "Taxation and the Size Distribution of Income" (1959), "How Much Does the American System of Transfers Do for the Poor?" (1966), and "Public and Private Transfers as Social Process" (1969). Part C grows out of "Approaches to the Reduction of Poverty" (1964), "Ends and

Means in the War on Poverty" (1966), "Steps To Remove Poverty from America" (1969), and "Transfer Approaches to Income Redistribution" (1969).

Other papers from which excerpts were drawn in various parts of the book include the following: "Income and Welfare: A Review Article" (1963), "Poverty and Affluence of American Labor" (1966), "What We Have Learned about Poverty" (1968), and "Transfer and Redistribution as Social Process" (1969).

Permission to quote extensively from earlier writings published by Yale University Press (*Poverty Amidst Affluence*, edited by Leo Fishman) and *The Quarterly Journal of Economics* (Harvard University Press) is gladly acknowledged.

In preparing this book, the author has been much helped by the research and editorial assistance of the following members of the staff of the Institute for Research on Poverty: Felicity Skidmore, Joyce D. Fishbane, Benton P. Gillingham, Nancy Kreinberg, and Ann Jacobs. Production was facilitated by Pat Johnson and Catherine Ersland.

He has gained valuable counsel from associates at the Institute, particularly Harold W. Watts, and from colleagues in the Department of Economics. He benefited from critical reviews of a rough draft of the manuscript by Robert A. Levine, Sar Levitan, Alice Rivlin, James Tobin, and Adam Yarmolinsky. His students in recent classes in a course on income and wealth distribution have served as a test group for many of the ideas put forth in this book.

CONTENTS

LIST OF TABLES

LIST OF FIGURES

Figure

PART A

The Antipoverty Goal in Historical Perspective

Chapter 1

THE POLICY BACKGROUND

Poverty reduction is both an end in itself and a means toward such other important purposes of our political economy as economic progress and political democratization. Many decades of concern with poverty and inequality lie behind the first explicit statement of a national anti-poverty goal. This statement was made in 1964, when President Johnson pointed the nation toward a goal of moving all American families and unrelated individuals above income levels of $3000 and $1500 respectively (in 1962 prices). In 1947 32 percent of families were below the $3000 line, but by 1957 23 percent, and by 1967 only 13 percent were below that line. Continuing that rate of decrease would bring the poverty rate to near zero by 1980. The goal of accelerating that rate was implied by the President's statement that "we cannot and need not wait for the gradual growth of the economy to lift this fifth of our Nation above the poverty line." It is consistent with the above to think of the goal in terms of narrowing the poverty income gap—the aggregate amount by which the income of all the poor falls short of $3000 per family—which totaled $14 billion in 1959 and $10 billion in 1967. If this gap could be narrowed by $1 billion per year, the aim of the war on poverty would be reached before 1980.

RECENT STATEMENTS ON THE POSSIBILITY OF ELIMINATING POVERTY

President Johnson's statement of the goal to eliminate poverty was a reflection of a widely held view of its possibility. Robert H. Bremner says, "During the first two centuries of the country's development Americans took it for granted that the majority of men would be poor."[1] However, between 1830 and 1917 Americans both "discovered" poverty and gained hope that it could be abolished. "In contrast to the peoples

---
[1]*From the Depths: The Discovery of Poverty in the United States* (New York University Press, 1956), p. 3.

of less fortunate lands, who have accepted poverty as inevitable, Americans have tended to regard it as an abnormal condition[. Their] confidence in the eradicability of poverty has . . . been a dynamic force for reform in the United States."[2] Valdemar Carlson identifies this with the belief in human progress that became a social creed in the nineteenth century. He points out that "paradoxically, the belief in the total abolition of poverty was held by both the opponents and the proponents of generous and humane treatment of the poor. Both endorsed the general principle that if the environment were properly changed and manipulated, poverty could be made to disappear."[3]

This hope must have been based upon observation of progress. However, during this period there were few studies of the scope of poverty. In 1892 Jacob Riis estimated that from 20 to 30 percent of New York City's population lived in penury. Robert Hunter guessed that 12 to 24 percent of all Americans lived in poverty in 1904. In making his rough calculations, Hunter suggested a guideline of $460 in annual income for a family of five in an urban setting, and $300 for the South. But in 1906 Father John A. Ryan set a poverty line of $600. The fact that this was above the median wage for adult males suggests that he thought about half of all families had incomes below what was required for "health and self-respect." The staff director of the Industrial Commission's investigation of 1916 thought that from one-third to one-half of all wage earnings were "inadequate."

However, bright hopes were being expressed. In 1910 Robert W. Bruere declared, "There is wealth enough in the world to make successful war on poverty." In 1914 Jacob H. Hollander asserted, "Now, in our own day, the conquest of poverty looms up as an economic possibility, definitely within our reach—if only society desires it sufficiently and will pay enough to achieve it." In 1928 President Herbert Hoover concluded that the United States was nearer to the abolition of poverty and the fear of want than humanity had reached before. It was a slogan in the United States during the 1920s that we had achieved permanent prosperity and could look forward to a chicken in every pot and a car in every garage. By the present standards of three thousand 1962 dollars of income per family, almost half of Americans were poor at that time, and a rising percentage were poor in the early thirties. It was not until 1947 that the poor were less than one-third of the population by present-day measures. However, using a different standard, Franklin D. Roosevelt in 1936 spoke of one-third of a nation as "ill-housed, ill-clad and

---

[2]Ibid., p. xi.
[3]*Economic Security in the United States* (New York: McGraw-Hill, 1962), p. 26.

ill-nourished," but said he foresaw a time when the lowest standards of living would be high above the subsistence level.

The spectacular recovery from the stagnation of the 1930s during World War II and the continued economic growth through the 1950s gave rise to the general appreciation of an "economic miracle." This euphoria was heightened by the insight that there had been an "income revolution" during 1938–44, in which the highest income groups had lost ground (relatively), in terms of both pre- and post-tax income. It was widely claimed that not only income but wealth was more evenly distributed and that America was becoming a "people's capitalism." This no doubt contributed to a general lack of concern about poverty.

In 1958 John Kenneth Galbraith characterized the society as affluent and beyond the bane of "general poverty."[4] He asserted that an unspecified number of people who remained poor were unlikely to benefit from further economic growth and would need specialized attention. They were, according to Galbraith, the "island poor"—those in isolated pockets of poverty—and the "case poor"—those who suffered from personal handicaps. This assertion was to prove controversial, but Galbraith's best-selling book, *The Affluent Society,* did bring poverty back into the limelight.

Two studies for the Joint Economic Committee of Congress pointed to the persistence of poverty in the prosperous postwar years. One of these studies, done by the present author in 1959, stated that the share of the population in "low-income status" had fallen from 26 percent in 1947 to 19 percent in 1957. Hearings before the Joint Economic Committee, and the work of Senator Paul A. Douglas and others on the Committee, may be said to have prepared Congress for the Economic Opportunity Act. Many other studies were conducted under private auspices. Considerable new information on the nature of the poverty population and their sources of income was added by a sample survey carried out by James N. Morgan, Martin David, Wilbur J. Cohen, and Harvey Brazer.[5] Michael Harrington produced a convincing portrait of the poor in his popular book, *The Other America.*[6] One of his themes was that much of the poverty in the nation had become "invisible" to the typical citizen. Numerous studies and journalistic accounts of such special groups in poverty as the migrant workers, those in depressed communities in Appalachia, and the aged added to public awareness that there was a substantial number of

---

[4]*The Affluent Society* (Boston: Houghton Mifflin, 1958).

[5]*Income and Welfare in the United States* (New York: McGraw-Hill, 1962).

[6]*The Other America: Poverty in the United States* (New York: Macmillan, 1962).

poor people in this country even twenty years after the end of the Great Depression.

These books and articles carried an optimistic message about the possibility of overcoming poverty. Many of them declared that poverty had become an anachronism. Hence the ground was prepared for President Johnson to call for the elimination of poverty.

BRITISH BACKGROUND

President Johnson's declaration of a war on poverty came out of a developing conviction that the goal was attainable. That conviction, in turn, was promoted by a long record of successful economic and social development in western countries.

The reduction of the percentage of the population in poverty, as distinguished from mere alleviation and regulation of distress, was powered by the economic growth arising out of technological change and extension of the market. The great conversion to a free-contract, open-market system may be thought of as the dominant emphasis in a centuries-long war on poverty. This struck off the bonds that held some people in subservient status, restricted opportunity to a select few, and saddled others with paternalistic responsibilities.

It is a matter of controversy among historians whether the extent and/or the intensity of poverty temporarily increased in England with the Industrial Revolution, generally dated from 1750. Population growth, migration to the cities, and changes in the life-style of the poor cloud the issue. It is possible that there was a reduction in the extent of poverty simultaneous with a decline in the standards of care for those remaining in poverty.[7] But in long retrospect it seems clear that the number of non-poor grew faster than the number of poor starting sometime after 1750.

The great conversion referred to did not lead to implementation of the full logic of the market in England—or anywhere else, for that matter. British practice during the American colonial period reflected a curious combination of market and pre-market thinking,[8] exemplified by the Poor

---

[7]Brian Tierney, in his study of *Medieval Poor Law* (Berkeley: University of California Press, 1959), concludes that "the poor were better looked after in England [in the thirteenth century] than in any subsequent century until the present one" (p. 3).

[8]Samuel Mencher, *Poor Law to Poverty Program: Economic Security Policy in Britain and the United States* (Pittsburgh: University of Pittsburgh Press, 1967).

Laws of 1531 and 1601, the 1662 Law of Settlement and Removal, and the 1795 Speenhamland system of minimum income allowances. On the one hand, they set forth the idea that no able-bodied person should be granted relief. On the other, they discouraged such a person from leaving his parish to find work. While the labor market was becoming national in scope, the central government dealt with beggars, rogues, rufflers, and vagabonds by beating their backs until bloody and returning them to their place of settlement, wherein the paternalistic ethic of feudalism was expected to come into play. If necessary, the parish could set them on work relief or, as in the case of Speenhamland, supplement wages to a minimum standard related to family size.

While the Poor Laws established strong disincentives against pauperism and dependency, this was not the full story. For those unable to work, provisions were made. The aged were settled in cottages on the waste, children were apprenticed, and work houses, orphanages, asylums, and alms houses were maintained. Many other schemes for dealing with the poor were in the air in early nineteenth-century England. Jeremy Bentham favored Houses of Industry which would improve upon John Cary's Corporation of the Poor in Bristol by aiming to reform and rehabilitate the poor while alleviating their distress. He favored special efforts to conserve and rescue the children of paupers. He saw the need for education and health care, assistance and insurance, and cooperative actions on the part of the self-maintaining poor. It is doubtful that any contemporary ideas about the poor would have seemed novel to Bentham's circle.[9]

In 1798 Bentham opined that in England "the multitude included under the denomination of the poor compose the bulk of the community—nineteen twentieths might perhaps be found to belong to that class." Less than a century later, Charles Booth estimated that only 30 percent of the people in London lived in poverty. In 1902 Sidney Webb said he thought it was fantasy to believe that anything short of sheer communism could abolish poverty. However, in 1909 Prime Minister David Lloyd George presented his budget to Parliament with the declaration, "This is a war budget for raising money to wage implacable warfare against poverty and squalidness. I cannot help believing that before this generation has passed away, we shall have advanced a great step towards that good time when poverty and the degradation which always follow in its camp, will be as remote to the people of this country as the wolves

---

[9]See *The Works of Jeremy Bentham,* Vol. VIII (Edinburgh: London, Simpkin, Marshall & Co., 1843), p. 395.

which once infested its forests." (This illustrates the commonly stated generalization that in matters of social policy, the United States follows England with a time-lag of fifty years.)

The basic policies toward poverty in seventeenth- and eighteenth-century England were free contract, cautious extension of education and of suffrage, work relief for the able-bodied poor, and work houses for the nonable-bodied paupers. And this was the heritage of colonial America, within which, except for slaves, individualism was nourished without restraints from a feudalistic past.

FOUR STRATEGIES AGAINST POVERTY IN AMERICA

A wide variety of efforts—not all of them primarily intended as anti-poverty measures—have been and are still being made in America to move people out of poverty, to prevent retreat into poverty, and to meet the needs of those in poverty. All of them may be ordered and comprehended under the heading "four strategies against poverty." The first of these is to establish and facilitate the working of a market system aimed at economic growth and maintenance of high employment. The second is to adapt the system to the needs of the poor. The third is to change the poor and adapt them to the system. The fourth is to relieve the distress of the poor. (It is not our intention here to suggest that the reader think of these as alternatives. They are in large part complementary strategies.)

Make the Market Work

This strategy defines and redefines the basic institutions of property, contract, and market organization. From the outset, American governments played a strong role in determining the structure and operation of the private economy. They have functioned not only as rulemakers but also as active promoters of business. They have affected the pattern of land use, the system of transport and communication, and the advance of science and technology. Governments have been active suppliers of health and education services. They have sought to offset the business cycle. The trend has been toward more governmental efforts to make the system work. Perhaps the most dramatic example of this is the use of monetary and fiscal policy to minimize unemployment.

Adapt the System to the Needs of the Poor

It is meaningful—though perhaps not very useful in practice—to draw a line separating the general economic activities of government from those which are aimed at adapting the "natural" or "preexisting" market system to serve better the needs and interests of the poor. Historically, such adaptation has been wrapped in the process of extending suffrage and developing a common citizenship. The most dramatic example of such adaptation is the abolition of slavery. The Homestead Act is another striking case, and the Freedmen's Bureau of the Reconstruction period was an early antipoverty agency.

Less spectacularly, the courts and legislatures are constantly modifying rights and obligations which bear upon opportunities and security for the poor. The law of property, of torts, and of contracts, as well as criminal law, are relevant. They touch basic matters of family responsibility and employer liability, and regulate transactions between buyer and seller, landlord and renter, debtor and creditor. An early example of a move in the balance of rights and obligations in favor of the poor is that of mechanics' lien laws; later examples are bankruptcy and usury laws, industrial safety codes, pure food and drug legislation, railroad and utility regulation, housing ordinances, the regulation of employment exchanges, and antidiscrimination laws. Regulation of the labor market, by first permitting and later encouraging collective bargaining and also by limiting individual bargaining in terms of such matters as child labor, minimum wages, and hours of work; and regulation of minimum prices, via resale price maintenance and agricultural price supports, are frequently justified as measures to meet needs of the poor. Another adaptation of the system which is built on similar considerations (more specifically, on the doctrine of social fault) is social insurance, whereby the employer and the consumer are drawn into arrangements to insure workers against the risk of industrial accident, unemployment, disability, old age, or premature death.

A still different adaptation to the needs of the poor is a shift from regressive to progressive taxation. Other examples are found in tariff and immigration policies. (Immigration was particularly singled out by nineteenth- and early twentieth-century observers as a cause of poverty; not only because many of the immigrants were poor, but [it was alleged] they pulled down the wages of all.) It is perhaps unnecessary to point out that adaptations which are nominally or originally introduced to serve the interest of the poor may not actually serve that purpose, and some (but of course not all) may do so only at the cost of reduced national product.

Our history in these matters of adapting the system has been for responsibility to swing from private to public groups, from local to state to federal government, and from the judicial to the legislative branch of government with increasing use of the specialized administrative commission or agency.

Adapt the Poor to the Market

A third broad strategy against poverty which we have followed is to adapt the poor to the market system and to improve their ability to seize opportunities to earn incomes. The effort has been to change the attitudes, values, motivations, and life-style of the poor and to develop their potential productivity.

Schools, churches, "friendly visitors" from charitable organizations, professional social workers, volunteers in settlement houses, as well as labor unions and other self-help organizations have sought to induce change in the poor. In many cases this was by export of middle-class values and the Protestant ethic wherein morality and personal salvation were associated with economic success. The poor were exhorted to practice thrift, temperance, prudence, and self-discipline, and to be mobile and "go west." Homeless children, wandering girls, and vagrants were counselled and in some cases assisted to seek new environments and regular employment. The new scientific philanthropy of the 1890s involved casework methods for helping the poor find a way to independence via family services, medical help, and inspirational example.

A different emphasis in changing the poor calls for broad services for the whole community of the poor. These include schools, libraries, informational services, hospitals, maternal and child clinics, nurseries, public housing, recreational facilities, and sanitary and other environmental improvements. In some cases this has meant extension of generally available services; in others it has meant especially modified services that were related to distinctive needs. Some of these services have not only been offered but compelled, as in the case of school attendance.

In this general field of "adapting the poor" the trend has been toward increasing emphasis upon services, again, with a swing from private and voluntary efforts over to those carried on by public agencies. The emphasis on services has not been without its critics. Some argue that services without changes in attitudes on the part of recipients do little good; other assert that if incomes were maintained, then the free services would not be necessary.

Relieve the Distress of the Poor

The fourth strategy has often been thought of as the residual one, although in some formulations of the problem it is either complementary or alternative to the other strategies. The history of our efforts to relieve distress of the poor begins with English experience in the colonies.

The American heritage of English poor law administration dictated an emphasis upon indoor as opposed to outdoor relief, only work relief—and that at less than prevailing wages—to able-bodied family heads, private as opposed to public responsibilities for emergency need, and local as opposed to central government decisionmaking. Making families and local governments responsible for relief was designed to discourage begging and vagrancy. Traditionally the community sought to protect itself against baneful influences of pauperism and degeneracy by such measures as isolation of the poor and denial of the right to vote or to marry.

This harsh poor law practice was slowly modified by a gradual increase in the number of categories of poor given special consideration. Veterans, the blind, insane, widows, children, aged, disabled, and depression unemployed have been singled out for more favorable treatment. Federal participation was slow in coming and was not broad in scope until the 1930s. To this day, public assistance programs retain a strong degree of localization, and general (i.e., noncategorical) assistance is not shared federally.

The old-fashioned term "relief" is being replaced by the more neutral characterizations of "transfer payment" and "nonfactor income." The distinction between public assistance and social insurance is becoming less clear, and there are several live proposals for "minimum income guarantees" and "comprehensive Social Security plans."[10] The fourth strategy should not, therefore, be considered a relic. It may be the wave of the future in the poverty war.

American history may be interpreted as a recounting of alternating interest in and experiment with the four strategies. If the early nineteenth century was a time of special attention to strategy 1 (making the system work), then later in the century was the time for strategy 3 (changing the poor). Strategy 2 (adapting the system to the poor) was emphasized in the early part of the twentieth century and again, along

---

[10]For an insightful discussion of historical trends in these matters, see Eveline M. Burns, "Social Security in Evolution: Towards What?" Proceedings of the Seventeenth Annual Meeting, Industrial Relations Research Association, 1964 (Madison, Wisconsin).

with strategy 4 (relieving distress), in the 1930s. Strategies 1 and 3 were given high priority in the 1950s and 1960s. It appears that strategy 4 may be stressed in the 1970s.

HOW THE ANTIPOVERTY GOAL RELATES TO OTHER ECONOMIC GOALS

The foregoing discussion argues that poverty reduction has long been an *implicit* goal in this country and that responsibility for achieving it has been drifting upward to the level of the federal government. However, it was a significant departure to state the goal explicitly and to identify it as a *national* goal. It may help us to see how much of a departure it was to note that poverty reduction is one of the relatively few "performance" goals enunciated by a President.

American economic goals may be classified into three types, namely "process goals," "overall performance goals," and "specific uses of output goals." Much discussion of economic goals has to do with processes. The pure types of economic process are tradition, market, and central direction.[11] The American economy's processes are a mix of these three. Yet the greater part of our value load is supportive of market processes and the individualism associated with them. Thus the Employment Act specifies that the employment and production goals are to be pursued "in a manner calculated to foster and promote free competitive enterprise and the general welfare." In our society the powers of government are limited, and success or failure in reaching economic objectives turns on the energies and initiative of our citizens in their capacities as business-men, farmers, workers, and consumers. Government provides a basic framework within which choices are to be made, sometimes limiting the range of the permissible, sometimes enlarging the range of the feasible. Maximizing the free choices effectively open to all individuals is the basic aim of economic policy in a democracy where ultimate value is the integrity and dignity of the individual human being.

In the pure-market rhetoric, the goal of developing worthwhile human beings is realizable only where individuals are free to make their own decisions and to bear the responsibility for those decisions. The prime values are freedom and opportunity. Novelty and change are facilitated: security and familiar ways of doing things are downgraded. Rewards go to the quick and the responsive rather than to the loyal and

---

[11]These concepts are discussed by Robert Heilbroner in *The Making of Economic Society* (Englewood Cliffs, N.J.: Prentice-Hall, 1962).

the old-fashioned. The consistent spokesman for the market process defends it in terms of character building rather than as a way to build GNP, and he would stand by it even though it could be demonstrated that it did less for national production than central direction. He believes that the striving is more important than the achieving. In this system of thought, economic goals of the nation are the sum of the goals of individuals, and whatever production and consumption patterns arise are, by definition, the "right" patterns. They are validated by consumer sovereignty on the one hand and competitive discipline on the other hand.

It is commonplace to observe that we have departed from if indeed we were ever committed to, the pure market process.[12] The liberal system gave people not only the freedom to compete but also the freedom to combine. Americans have sought by means of tariffs, labor unions, trade and professional associations, and social legislation to moderate the rigors of the market. They have sought group security and limits on inequality of opportunity and condition. They have adapted the system to the needs of the poor in numerous ways, as we reviewed above. But in thus departing from the pure market process they have not gone far toward central direction. Decisions are made in a decentralized, pluralistic, checks-and-balances fashion, and no single person or group can act definitively on many issues.

Quite distinct from process goals are what we may define as overall performance goals. In point of time, these have been more emphasized recently than they were earlier. These goals are national rather than individual in character and involve aggregative considerations. As President Kennedy put it in his "economic myths" speech at Yale University in 1962, "The national interest lies in high employment and steady expansion of output, in stable prices and a strong dollar."[13] In that speech he urged that we not be doctrinaire about preferred processes in seeking ways to achieve important performance goals. These

---

[12]Jacob Viner observes that "in its ideology the American public . . . clings faithfully . . . to maxims and stereotypes of 19th Century laissez faire . . . but these are in large part merely semantic loyalties on our part, rather than operative rules for actual behavior." Viner goes on to say that our modern economy is formed by "unplanned responses to historical forces and political pressures." It does not have, he asserts, "an internally coherent and logically formulated philosophy" and is not guided by any "clear and widely accepted consensus as to where it is going or where it should go from here." "The United States as a Welfare State," in Edgar O. Edwards, ed., *The Nation's Economic Objectives* (Chicago: University of Chicago Press for Rice University, 1964), pp. 151–67.

[13]June 11, 1962. For an interesting discussion of the ideas set forth in this speech, see James Tobin, *National Economic Policy* (New Haven, Conn.: Yale University Press, 1966), chap. 4.

goals, he said, cannot be reached by "incantations from the forgotten past." He might also have said they cannot be reached by decentralized process alone. They require a strong head at the center. In 1964 President Johnson added to this list the goal of steadily reducing poverty.

It can be argued, of course, that these performance goals are supportive rather than destructive of our process goals, which, as we have said, are basically justified in terms of their contribution to freedom and challenge for individuals. Achievement of the performance goals enumerated may enlarge the range of choice and opportunity for individuals. On the other hand, a performance goal, e.g., the antipoverty goal, may be pursued in such a way that the process goals and other performance goals are lost.

Overall performance goals are more concrete than process goals, and what we can call "specific use of output goals" are more concrete than either of the other types. Here we are talking about such things as better housing, trips to the moon, new urban transit systems, new regional medical centers, and new types of pre- and postschool training. We are talking, as the National Planning Association would have us do, of a national economic budget which shows all expenditure, private and public, classified by object and purpose.[14] Going beyond process goals and performance goals is justified by the assertion that there is a national as well as an individual and local interest in the achievement of high standards in education, health, transportation, and recreation, as well as in research and development, and a need to set priorities in order to accomplish a preferred part of the specific use of output goals.

It is not necessary to point out that statement of a goal implies a plan, and identification of priorities implies a method. Plans and methods for implementing these specific uses of output goals may conflict with process goals and overall performance goals. In particular, they may require new roles for government. Some of these specific uses of output goals relate to the performance goals. For example, improvement of budgets for health, education, and income maintenance may contribute to the reduction of poverty. Below, in chapter 6, "Change in Income Redistribution," we offer an accounting scheme for identifying how specific uses of output bear on poverty reduction.

It would appear, then, that we have an abundance of economic goals. We have goals concerning the processes of the economy, its overall performance and the specific uses of output. Over the years these goals

---

[14]Leonard A. Lecht, *Goals, Priorities, and Dollars* (New York: Free Press, 1966).

have gained in specificity and in the degree to which they are national in character. These economic goals of contemporary Americans come from the profound moral insights of the founders of western civilizations, and also from the revolutions of recent centuries. The goals of today are not only restatements of goals of earlier generations, since the latter have been modified by particular historical forces and political pressures. Some weight must also be given to contemporary reformers, social accountants,[15] and experts as originators of goals. Among these experts are social scientists, whose thought on the subject of inequality is reviewed in the following section.

In taking up this review, we are not trying to explain how the Economic Opportunity Act came to passage. A full discussion of that would take us in rather different directions and would emphasize the multiplicity of goals in that legislation, of which the antipoverty goal is only one.[16] Rather, in the pages that follow we concentrate on the relationship between scholarly work and the emergence of the goal of eliminating income poverty.

---

[15]As Bertrand de Jouvenel says, "Designers of statistics are indeed philosophers, however unwilling to claim the name, and are fully aware that different aspects of reality can be lit up if alternative sets of concepts are used" (cited by Bertram M. Gross and Michael Springer, "New Goals for Social Information," *The Annals* 373 (September 1967), 209. In a similar vein, "John Kenneth Galbraith has noted the indispensable role of statisticians in modern societies, which seem never to do anything about problems until they learn to measure them, that being the special province of those applied mathematicians. Statistics are used as mountains are climbed: because they are there." Daniel P. Moynihan, *Maximum Feasible Misunderstanding* (New York: Free Press, 1969), p. 30.

[16]For good legislative histories of this act see Sar Levitan, *The Great Society's Poor Law* (Baltimore: Johns Hopkins Press, 1969); and James L. Sundquist, *Politics and Policy: The Eisenhower, Kennedy, and Johnson Years* (Washington, D.C.: Brookings Institution, 1968), chap. 4.

Chapter 2

BACKGROUND OF SOCIAL SCIENCE
THOUGHT ON INEQUALITY

The antipoverty goal is related to broader concern for the pattern of income distribution, the sharing of public services, and the limits on inequality of opportunity. Correlatively, the study of poverty is a subtopic in the study of inequality. Interestingly, there are changes in income distribution which affect only the upper and middle ranks of the population and do not alter the income share of the lowest. One branch of social criticism envisions a "power line" near the top of the income and wealth distribution, while another has focused on a "poverty line" near the bottom. Poverty reduction means "leveling up" the bottom of the income distribution rather than restraining the power and influence of the very rich. The costs of this may be borne by the middle rather than the upper income groups. However, as a practical matter, the benefits of many antipoverty programs will have to extend to the near-poor. There is some rate of poverty reduction which, given a rate of economic growth, will increase the share of total income going to the lowest ranking 10 or 20 percent of the population, and may thereby result, at least temporarily, in a narrowing of overall income inequality. There is, then, a logical connection between poverty and inequality.

In a broad sense, President Johnson's enunciation of a distributional goal may be interpreted as the outcome of a long trend in social science toward a more favorable reception for the idea of reducing inequalities among people. This interpretation is plausible even though the previous two decades had seen a marked decline in scholarly interest in distributional questions. The mainstream of economic thought was directed toward the goals of economic stability and growth. Economists and sociologists had lost confidence in their ability to specify why one income distribution was better than another. "Poverty" was no longer a fashionable word among academics. In 1964 Theodore W. Schultz observed that "poverty, for want of a theory, is lost in economics notwithstanding all of the statistics that show the size distributions of personal income . . . there is no integrated body of economic knowledge and no agenda of economic hypotheses to get at important economic questions about poverty."[1]

In spite of the decline of interest noted, it is relevant for us here to review the traditional arguments for and against narrowing economic differences.[2] These may be classified as (1) value-judgment statements concerning the desirability or undesirability of a particular degree of inequality, (2) consequential propositions which may be used to argue for or against equalization in terms of the alleged results of one or another pattern of inequality, and (3) causal propositions which seek to explain what causes a given pattern of inequality to come into being and to change, and which are often important in argument for or against equalization.

In the section which follows we review recent trends in thought on these three points and on a fourth, namely why individuals or groups are disposed to favor or oppose lessening of economic inequalities.

THE VALUE-JUDGMENT LEVEL

This is the level on which argument proceeds by definition. A policy to reduce inequality is advocated because diminished inequality is asserted to be, by definition, a necessary part of a more ideal social arrangement. Thus a straightforward value judgment is made without reference to consequences. Conversely, equalization may be opposed, or increases in the degree of inequality advocated, because the ideal society is visualized as that in which a particular pattern of considerable inequality obtains.

The recent history of Western nations reveals an increasingly widespread adoption of the idea that substantial equality of social and economic conditions among individuals is a good thing. The roots of egalitarian thought are deep in Western civilization. Yet it is undoubtedly correct to label as a modern phenomenon the sweep of such thinking into the practical arena of political, social, and economic affairs.

Egalitarianism has advanced on a moving front, from concern with legal equality, to religious equality, to political and economic equality.

---

[1]"Investing in Poor People: An Economist's View," *American Economic Review* 55 (May 1965), 510.

[2]This chapter is essentially a shortened version of Robert J. Lampman, "Recent Thought on Egalitarianism," *Quarterly Journal of Economics* 71 (May 1957), 234–66. The reader who is interested in more extensive references to the literature should consult that article.

Assertions of small-group superiority have been transmuted into demands for extensions of privileges to larger groups. Thus equality has become a working principle in a growing number of fields and among increasing numbers of people. This extension of the concept as well as the sharing of citizenship gives considerable basis for concluding, with David Thomson, that "the most actively operative ideal of our own time is equality. . . ."[3]

The egalitarian question is different for every generation. Particularly, the question now focuses upon economic inequalities. Economic equality in its broadest and most abstract sense means the absolutely equal division among all human beings of each of many kinds of material wealth and income and all that is associated with wealth and income, such as welfare, power, and prestige.

It is obvious that all these "goods" cannot be equally distributed simultaneously. No one seriously proposes that this be attempted. Rather, attention is centered on one at a time. On the consumer side equalization may refer to equal meeting of needs, equal satisfaction, or equal protection against hazards to economic security. On the producer side it may refer to equal effort or disutility of work, equal opportunity in the economic "game," or equal participation in and power to influence economic decisionmaking. It is worth a special note that equality of opportunity is not necessarily consistent with, and may be antithetical to, equality of condition.

To answer the question whether economic equalization is a "good thing" or not requires first that the question be asked. This means that

---

[3]*Equality* (Cambridge, England: Cambridge University Press, 1949), p. 137. Interest in equalization has differed by countries. Thomson notes (p. 23), "The links between autocratic centralized forms of government and the development of egalitarianism, both in theory and in practice, are close." On the other hand, in the United States equality has long been a significant word; see T. V. Smith, *The American Philosophy of Equality* (Chicago, 1927). The significance of equality in America has been observed by those of widely differing points of view De Tocqueville concluded: "The more I advanced in the study of American society, the more I perceived that this equality of condition is the fundamental fact from which all others seemed to be derived, and the central point at which all my observations terminated" (*Democracy in America* I [New York: Harper & Row, 1966], Introduction, 1). Harold J. Laski identified egalitarianism as "the central thread in the American tradition [against which] no one has yet been able to make a successful frontal attack" (*The American Democracy* [New York: Viking Press, 1948], p. 718). The editors of *Fortune* called "the great ideal of Equality, the fundamental 'tendency' of American life . . . [among] the most valuable contributions we have to offer the world" ("The American Way of Life," *Fortune* [February 1951], p. 191).

the pattern of economic inequality must be recognized as a manipulable variable. The beginnings of social science are marked by the frank recognition of all social institutions, including wealth and income distribution, as variables that can be engineered. The experimental approach to social problems opened up the way to speculative thought on many social questions. Political economists have often asked leading questions of normative character. Smith asked: Is laissez-faire better than state direction of economic activity? Ricardo asked: Which is the best functional income distribution? Marx asked: What is the best relationship among classes and the state as regards the distribution of property rights? Bentham asked: What is the best degree of inequality among persons in the distribution of wealth and income?

Defining the egalitarian question requires more than raising it and recognizing that the personal income distribution is a manipulable variable. It requires further that the question be placed high on the agenda for current solution. This the discipline of political economy has been slow to do.

Bentham insisted that the question of equity could be treated only after stability and progress were assured. The unfolding of the Benthamite tradition would seem to dictate that as other problems come nearer to solution the egalitarian question would be more seriously considered. This unfolding is perhaps best seen in the recent willingness of economists to support such egalitarian policies as progressive taxation and "welfare state" expenditures. It is also to be seen in the increasing attention given to the facts of economic inequality (particularly personal income inequality) in economics textbooks.[4]

While contemporary economists insist upon asking the egalitarian question, accord a good deal of attention to the facts of economic inequality, and take policy positions on many programs which will reduce inequality, there are remarkably few explicit definitional statements made on the egalitarian question as such. There is a hiatus between asking the question and assuming a policy position on programs. The overleaping of the explicit value-judgment statement is noted in two essays in this field. Stigler observes that:

---

[4]Martin Bronfenbrenner, in "Radical Economics in America: A 1970 Survey," *Journal of Economic Literature* 8 (September 1970), 747–67, notes the stress by the new radicals on income distribution. He quotes John Weeks as saying: "The overriding reality of the American economy is inequality—inequality of income, inequality of power, inequality with regard to the ability to determine one's own life. *Inequality is what economics should be all about*" (p. 756).

Economists as a class have always been opposed to inequality of income, and also to equality. The summary, however, does not disclose the major shift of attitude within the last generation [because] more recently (since Marshall), the desire for equality has grown strong. Every policy is scrutinized for its effect on the distribution of income, and the results of this scrutiny weigh heavily in the final judgment of the desirability of the policy. A growing number of economists indeed argue implicitly that no other injury equals in enormity that of large differences in income.[5]

Blum and Kalven uncover the hiatus in a rather different way. When economists are faced with a policy question such as the desirability of progressive income taxation, they do not ordinarily give an explicit value-judgment statement on the question of equality. Thus Blum and Kalven find that:

Although there is a very considerable literature on equality, and progressive taxation occupies some role in it, in the literature on progression there has been surprisingly little discussion of the equality issue.[6]

Few economists have taken a stand on the value-judgment level as forthrightly as Simons, who wrote:

The case for drastic progression in taxation must be rested on the case against inequality—on the ethical or aesthetic judgment that the prevailing distribution of wealth and income reveals a degree (and/or kind) of inequality which is distinctly evil or unlovely.[7]

Explanations of the apparent unwillingness of many economists to make explicit value judgments on the egalitarian question are to be found both in the changing nature of the egalitarian question and in

---

[5]George J. Stigler, "The Economists and Equality," *Five Lectures on Economic Problems* (New York: Macmillan, 1950), pp. 1–11. Alfred Marshall died in 1924.

[6]Walter J. Blum and Harry Kalven, Jr., *The Uneasy Case for Progressive Taxation* (Chicago: University of Chicago Press, 1953), p. 70. These authors treat a long list of consequential arguments for and against progression and conclude that most of the arguments are shaky reeds on which to lean, and that "the case [for progression] has stronger appeal when progressive taxation is viewed as a means of reducing economic inequalities" (p. 104).

[7]Henry Simons, *Personal Income Taxation* (Chicago: University of Chicago Press, 1938), pp. 18–19.

attitudes of social scientists toward *any* statement on the value-judgment level.

The egalitarian question has changed over time from a general question to a multipartite and more specific question. The very fact that the question has thus changed reflects a major shift in emphasis. The asking of the more particular question implicitly carries an answer to the first. The affirmative answer to the general question about equalization is so generally and so subconsciously given, so much a part of our culture-load, that any further value-judgment statement seems redundant. Agreement that equality is a good thing has become so general that denial may be entered only indirectly, as in George Orwell's *Animal Farm,* where it was reported, "We are all equal here, only some of us are more equal than others." Thus it is at least a plausible explanation of the hiatus that the moving front of egalitarianism has carried us beyond the value-judgment level.

There are two other possible explanations for the unwillingness of economists to make explicit value judgments on the question of equalization. These have to do with views of the appropriate role of scholars in forming policy. Both the conservative view of the role of the intellectual and the logical-positivist view of the role of the scientist have operated as restraints on the value-judgment level.

In the historical context of the last one hundred and fifty years, egalitarians have generally (with important exceptions) been in a position of advocating positive steps toward equalization rather than opposing newly created or proposed inequalities. The Burkean conservative's response to this is that agreement on social arrangements is difficult to come by and cannot be contrived by intellectual planners since rational discussion and social experiment are not to be trusted as ways to promote agreement. In this view intellectuals should not lead in change, but should merely accommodate such changes as great shifts in time and circumstance require.[8] To the extent that equalization measures become part of a generally accepted and deeply rooted program, it becomes easier for a conservative to support them, not because he thinks equality is a good thing, but because equalization has become part of the social agreement.

The logical positivist has another reason for charging that value judgment on the egalitarian question is inappropriate for the political

---

[8]A present-day disciple of Burke asserts that "the role of social science lies not in the formulation of social policy, but in the measurement of its results" (Daniel P. Moynihan, *Maximum Feasible Misunderstanding: Community Action in the War on Poverty* [New York: Free Press, 1969], p. 193).

economist. A question that asks which distribution is "best" is not subject to a "scientific" answer, since an answer to what is "best" is not possible to prove or disprove by an observable, objectively measurable operation. A nonoperational proposition is a poetic or emotive statement. While an intellectual may, of course, consider the normative question (thus the logical positivist differs from the conservative position) he will not be a "scientist" in so doing. (This is an interesting turnabout in that the positivist movement in social science raised the question of what is the best income distribution, and the latter-day positivists dismiss that question from social science.) The persuasive definition of "science" then suggests that one can be an egalitarian and/or a scientific economist, but one cannot be a scientific egalitarian on the value-judgment level. This level is the natural habitat of poets, politicians, and priests. When the economist enters it he must check his scientific guns at the door. His scientific standing will be unimpaired by "technical" advocacy concerning equalization measures, but that is possible only on the consequential level.

A consistent extension of logical-positivist thinking is to attempt to take economists out of the business of making value judgments altogether. One way to do this is to avoid talking about the "best" income distribution, that is, simply ignore the question. Another is to get others to make the value judgment on income distribution in the form of a "social welfare function."[9] However, the economist does not entirely escape making a value judgment by this method since he must evaluate the preferences of individuals and resolve contradictions among them in seeking to interpret "the community's" preference.[10]

THE CONSEQUENTIAL LEVEL

Statements on the value-judgment level are those which merely identify a given pattern of inequality with an ideal social arrangement. Such statements are purely normative in character. A person may advocate or oppose particular equalization measures simply because he likes a certain amount of inequality. However, most students want to have a reason for supporting or opposing equalization measures other than simple preference for equality or inequality. It is easy to conclude that egali-

---

[9]Cf. Schultz, "Investing in Poor People."

[10]Cf. Jerome Rothenberg, *The Measurement of Social Welfare* (Englewood Cliffs, N.J.: Prentice-Hall, 1961).

tarians are not really interested in equality at all. Thus Henry M. Oliver is struck by

> the consistency with which equality per se turns out not to be a major goal, in spite of egalitarian phrasing of arguments. Regardless of the type of equality considered, be it legal status, opportunity, income, wealth, or power, study suggests that the deeper interests of most professed egalitarians are rather in such matters as satisfactions, aesthetic achievements, personal character, fraternity, and the like.[11]

One step removed from value-judgment statements on the normative-nonnormative continuum are those which declare or imply that a stated pattern of inequality is good or bad because it is alleged that it will yield a particular consequence. Determination and prediction of consequence may, of course, be divorced from evaluation of those consequences. On the other hand, not all statements which are offered as consequential propositions are methodologically different from "mere" statements of preference.

The vast literature that bears on this subject shows arguments clustered around five consequential propositions.[12] These are: (1) the utilitarian proposition that equalization of incomes will lead to maximization of consumer satisfactions; (2) the "liberal" proposition that economic equalization will lead to the ideal allocation of power; (3) the "classical" proposition that inequality contributes to economic progress; (4) the Malthusian proposition that inequality results in (or is necessary to) cultural progress; (5) the sociological proposition that inequality is necessary to the working of a complex society.

We are not interested in analyzing and appraising these arguments as such. Rather, our concern is with identifying significant changes in emphasis accorded them. Especially striking are the shifts in the burden of proof which have been effected.

The utilitarian proposition has long played a leading role in consequential argument by egalitarians. After a long struggle to gain acceptance as an "economic" argument, this proposition is now widely discredited as a "nonscientific" proposition. As such it is pushed back to the value-judgment level of argument.

The utilitarian proposition is a conditional prediction of a conse-

---

[11]*A Critique of Socioeconomic Goals* (Bloomington: Indiana University Press, 1954), p. 100.

[12]Some readers will identify these propositions as speculations anterior to benefit-cost analyses.

quence. It says: If people have equal and identical experience of the diminishing marginal utility of money income, then an equal distribution of a given total of money income will yield the maximum total of individual utilities or satisfactions which it is possible to derive from that total of money income, all other things remaining the same. As long as the test of acceptability is logical truth or "reasonableness" or "plausibility," it is fair to say that the burden of proof lies with those who do not like the utilitarian conclusion. It is up to them to come up with a counter-proposition that is equally logical or more "reasonable" or "plausible." But a critical shift in the burden of proof takes place when the idea is introduced that the test of acceptability is empirical verification. If the utilitarian proposition is stripped of its conventional introduction, it becomes a "prediction" that reduction of inequality in the distribution of money incomes will result in an increase in the total of individual satisfactions, ceteris paribus. In order for a prediction to be verifiable the result must be (at least in principle) subject to an independently observable operation of testing. However, if satisfactions are defined as a purely subjective experience, then no interpersonal measurement or testing is possible. Hence it is alleged that the utilitarian proposition is nonoperational or nonverifiable in principle. Such statements merely express preferences and should be classified on the value-judgment level rather than on the consequential level. They are no different in kind from the forthright statement: "I like equality."

We have here a conflict between two kinds of argument. A "plausible" statement supported by a logical argument comes into conflict with the scientific test for truth. One response is to question the "plausibility" of the scientific argument. This may be done rather frivolously by posing the now familiar issue of being "roughly right" as against "precisely wrong." Another response, however, is to meet the logical positivists on their own ground by modifying the utilitarian proposition so that it will be verifiable. This can be done by "objectifying" the subject term of utility, taking it out of the subjective limbo and defining it in such a way as to make it measurable, recognizing that intensive magnitudes can be measured only by indication. The indicators to be used may be selected from among the alleged and observable consequences of income equalization, such as better health, greater educational opportunity, diminished class conflict, and so forth. There have been several suggestions for such objectification, but none of them has attracted a following of sufficient importance to significantly alter the course of the argument.

The utilitarian proposition is concerned with the consumer side of the economic equality issue. What we shall refer to as the liberal proposition is concerned with the producer side of the issue. More specifically, it is concerned with the power to make decisions regarding the course of producer activity.[13]

Concentration of the power to make decisions has concerned political economists for three reasons. One is the political concern that concentration of economic power is likely to accommodate political tyranny. A second and related point is that an economic arrangement in which there are only a few large agglomerations of power will limit the personality growth of most of the people by denying them the opportunity to develop their faculties. The third reason is fear that a heavily monopolized or privately collectivized economy will frustrate the ideal allocation of resources which, it is alleged, an atomistic competitive market structure will automatically yield.

On this question of concentration of economic power, reform thought has traditionally run in two directions. One is to accept collectivization but to "legitimize" it by state regulation or ownership and then to disperse the power by political democracy in control of the state. The other has been to oppose both private and public collectivization, preferring the dispersal of economic power that is involved in competition. These two types of structural reform have two models of egalitarian society in mind; the former related to equal voting power in deciding all issues, the latter related to a situation where every man is his own boss.

Any report of contemporary thought must record a gradual loss of interest in both the legitimization of collectivized decisionmaking and pursuit of atomistic competition. Particularly, the ideal of a nation of small farmers is in the shade. An intellectual rationale for a middle way is afforded by Galbraith's thesis of countervailing power, which at least partly succeeds in shifting the burden of proof from defenders of the status quo to the egalitarian reformers.[14] His work, which catches up the

---

[13]Several different distributions are involved here. One is the distribution of income among persons, income being thought of as an indication of the location of economic power. Similarly, the distribution of wealth among persons may be considered. On the other hand, organizations may be thought of as the loci of power, in which case personal income and wealth distribution is quite irrelevant since power attaches to office holding and effective control of organizations rather than income as such. A classification of individuals and organizations by degree of monopoly power is a still different type of "distribution."

[14]J. K. Galbraith, *American Capitalism* (Boston: Houghton Mifflin Co., 1952), and *The New Industrial State* (New York: New American Library, 1968). Also worth mentioning here is the idea of encouraging, by subsidy if necessary, poor people to become common stockholders in business corporations. See Louis O. Kelso and Patricia Hetter, *Two-Factor Theory: The Economics of Reality*, subtitled *How To Turn Eighty Million Workers into Capitalists on Borrowed Money and Other Proposals* (New York: Vintage Books, 1967).

strands of earlier institutional economists, urges the plausibility of accept-
ing concentrations of potential power as they appear, but expecting and
encouraging offsetting, neutralizing, or countervailing power concentrations. "Community action" by the poor may be an example of countervailing power.

Quite distinct from the above is the idea of leaving the structure of
the economy alone but taxing away part of the income, and hence the
economic power to decide, of the very rich. Whether this method of
reducing inequality will actually disperse or centralize economic power
is a controversial question. Henry C. Simons wrote:

> Thus I would suggest . . . not merely that progressive taxation
> is a sound and promising method for mitigating inequality, but
> that it is the only sound and promising method which has seri-
> ously been proposed and that other currently popular schemes
> are unsound technically and incompatible with the kind of total
> arrangements which we wish to preserve against the recently
> prevailing world trend.

One of the reasons why he preferred the taxation method was his belief
that no fundamental disturbance of the whole system is involved.[15]
On the other hand, Bertrand de Jouvenel, in viewing the contemporary
scene, sees income equalization programs as

> in effect, far less a redistribution of free income from the rich to
> the poorer . . . than a redistribution of power from the individual
> to the state.[16]

He considers centralization of power the major implication of redistribu-
tionist policies.

> Insofar as the state amputates higher incomes it must assume
> their saving and investment functions, and we come to the cen-
> tralization of investment. Insofar as the amputated higher
> incomes fail to sustain certain social activities, the State must
> step in, subsidize these activities, and preside over them. In-
> sofar as income becomes inadequate for the formation and ex-
> pense of those people who fulfill the more intricate of specialized
> social functions, the State must see to the formation and upkeep
> of this personnel. This results in a transfer of power from in-
> dividuals to officials, who tend to constitute a new ruling class
> as against that which is being destroyed.[17]

---

[15]*Personal Income Taxation*, pp. vi, 29.

[16]*Ethics of Redistribution* (Cambridge, England: Cambridge University
Press, 1951), p. 73.

[17]Ibid., pp. 77–78.

If the first consequential proposition deals with consumer-power income and the second with the power to decide, then the third deals with producer-contribution incomes. The proposition is that equalization of producer incomes by progressive income taxes and other measures will slow economic progress and diminish efficiency.

There are two separate but related subpropositions. One states that inequality of income is directly associated with the percentage of a given total output which will be saved. The percentage rate of saving is in turn said to be directly related to the economy's rate of growth via capital formation. Therefore, it is alleged, a reduction in the inequality of income will result in a reduction in the rate of progress. For lack of a better label, we shall call this the "classical proposition."

The second subproposition is this. Personal producer-contribution incomes arise out of factor prices. Differential factor prices are the means by which a free economy directs its factors out of idleness and into those industries, firms, and combinations and types of use within firms where they will perform the most highly valued functions. Equalizing such incomes is thus seen as blunting the edge of the price system. If factor incomes are made less unequal there is (it is alleged) less likelihood that resources will move where the market demands them; hence there will be less efficient response to changes in consumer demand and changes in producer technology.

Perhaps the way that these two subpropositions are phrased suggests the direction in which current thought must go. Whenever a statement is made that a "natural" arrangement gives the best result, or is both necessary and sufficient to the best result, it provides a field day for the critics, and almost any empirical finding is likely to appear to deny the statement. Thus, when the statement is made that the natural or existing pattern of inequality is necessary to and sufficient for the appropriate rate of saving and hence of investment, there are many exposed places for the critic to go to work. Is it necessary? Is it sufficient? What determines the appropriate rate of personal saving? May there not be a hiatus between a rate of saving and a rate of capital formation? May not a society progress more rapidly with a lower rate of saving?

Each of these questions has been asked and each has been answered in such a way as to move the burden of proof toward those who would defend the original statement. With reference to this proposition the egalitarians have been on the offensive, that is to say, the egalitarian is now in a position to demur when his proposal is attacked as one that will slow the rate of economic progress. His response is, "Your absolute statement is challenged as not being universally true, so I think it appropriate that you demonstrate the specific cost of my proposal." It is a nice shifting of the burden away from the egalitarian side of the argument.

The specific contributions which have accommodated this shift in burden are: (1) the Keynesian theory about the level of income determining saving rather than vice versa;[18] (2) historical and comparative studies of the degree of inequality, the rate of saving, and the rate of investment as related to the rate of progress; (3) analytical studies which tend to minimize the relative importance of private investment as the term is usually defined, and to emphasize other variables including social overhead and institutional patterns. Of special interest to this study is A. C. Pigou's line of thought that the rate of return on carefully managed investment in poor persons may exceed the normal rate of interest on capital invested in machinery and plant.

The argument that inequality is a necessary or a sufficient condition of economic progress via saving is taken much less seriously by the present generation of economists than by their forerunners. Much the same fate is met by the subproposition relating inequality of factor prices and economic efficiency. The proposition is usually stated in such general and absolute terms that it cannot be entirely validated empirically. Failure to withstand any particular test weakens the popularity of the general proposition. Several studies made indicate little if any loss of incentive to work and invest as a result of our present system of progressive income taxation. Such studies are important for the reason, among others, that they raise the question of where the burden of proof lies.

Contemporary economists, compared with earlier economists, are perhaps relatively less concerned about incentives for the rich and relatively more concerned about opportunities (rather than penalties) for the lower-income groups.[19] A growing company would share P. H.

---

[18]Many writers before Keynes urged the dangers of oversaving. Hobson was one, and he put inequality of incomes at the center of capitalism's internal difficulties. However, the harmonization of oversaving and egalitarian doctrines is indeed tenuous. In a period of sustained inflationary pressure Keynesian reasoning finds equality and efficiency antithetical.

[19]Consider the shift in opinion since Patrick Colquhoun wrote in *A Treatise on Indigence* (1806) as follows: "Without a large proportion of poverty there could be no riches, since riches are the offspring of labor, while labor can result only from a state of poverty. . . . Poverty therefore is a most necessary and indispensable ingredient in society, without which nations and communities could not exist in a state of civilization" (pp. 7–8). In contrast, Harold Watts suggested in 1968 that "it may seem absurd to suppose that the misery and squalor of the poor is the linchpin of the motivation system that elicits the diligent application and wise development of America's productive energies . . ." (unpublished, mimeo. paper).

Wicksteed's "anticipation that the reaction of a more even distribution upon the energies, tastes, and morals of the community would be such as to heighten rather than to lower the effectiveness of human effort."[20] Recent experience has led them to brush away the idea that there has to be some given amount of poverty. Most economists have long since given up the idea that a progressive society needs the existence of poverty to induce work and sobriety in the lower classes. (However, there is considerable disagreement about what would happen if all workers were given the option of working for, say, $3000, or receiving that amount as a guaranteed income.) Similarly, they consign to folk-lore the ideas that some are rich only because others are poor and exploited, that if none were poor then necessary but unpleasant jobs would go undone, that the middle class has a psychological need to exclude a minority from above-poverty living standards, and that poverty is a necessary concomitant of the unemployment which necessarily accompanies economic growth.

Indeed, contemporary writers are receptive to the idea that poverty, far from being functional in inducing productivity, is a dead weight on the economy and a cost to the rest of society. At present, the lowest fifth of the nation's population, ranked by income, produce about 3 percent of the total product, but they consume about 5 percent of it. In other words, if that fifth of the population were to disappear, national income would fall by only 3 percent and the product available for the remaining four-fifths would rise by 2 percent. Alternatively, eliminating poverty by increasing the productivity and earnings of the poor would produce a gain to the nation consisting of higher outputs and a lower outlay for "nuisance abatement" (presumably the need for police, fire, and public health protection is somewhat reduced by the rise in well-being of the poor). Further, there is a possible qualitative gain to the non-poor of the kind referred to by Wicksteed from the more complete integration of the population. Rather than having to live in a divided community of poor and nonpoor, they will find themselves in a more open community where all participate, compete, and cooperate. It is argued that almost all will benefit from the development of the talents and sense of responsibilities of the submerged poor.

---

[20]*Common Sense of Political Economy* (London: Macmillan and Co., Ltd., 1910), p. 655. Daniel P. Moynihan chides researchers for the fact that there is hardly any reliable information on how changes in income affect individual styles of life ("The Professors and the Poor," *Commentary* 46 (August 1968), 19–28, 26). In another context, he argues that "social science is at its weakest and its worst when it offers theories of individual or collective behavior which raise the possibility, by controlling certain inputs, of bringing about behavioral change" (Moynihan, *Maximum Feasible Misunderstanding,* p. 191).

However, egalitarians have generally taken care to explain their belief that some inequality of income is necessary for incentive purposes. The distinctions between "rents" and "costs" and between the "social surpluses" and "social costs" of Hobson are grist for the egalitarian's mill. Most egalitarians would agree with R. H. Tawney that "the real evil is capricious inequality and irresponsible power."[21] Significant differences are to be found, however, among the views of what is "capricious inequality." Here the distinction is drawn not in terms of the *degree* of inequality, but rather in terms of the *bases* of inequality. The concern is with the reasons for the rank-ordering of persons. (A prime case of this is the concern over income differences by race.)

The fourth consequential proposition is that moves toward economic equalization will diminish cultural achievement. Among economists Malthus is perhaps the leading spokesman for this cautionary speculation. He identified the bearers of the "seeds of culture" as the families of the landed aristocracy and enunciated this proposition as a part of a more general defense for that class. The argument was associated with a particular theory of the business cycle and was an integral part of a conservative, pessimistic view of the social process.

This proposition, and its surrounding philosophy, has never been popular among American authors, and we may note a continuing lack of interest in it. Perhaps it would be fair to say that modern economists have been more interested in extending cultural opportunity to more people than in excellence of cultural achievement. Most American social scientists withdraw in discomfort from Malthus' proposition, but few hesitate in advocating the right of all to share in and contribute to the Western cultural heritage. The success of egalitarianism is perhaps more apparent in this area than in any other, at least as far as America is concerned.

The fifth consequential proposition is that attempts to equalize will have important costs in terms of personal maladjustments and social friction. It notes a contradiction between the encouraging of equality of opportunity on the one hand and the requirement of social differentiation on the other.

Egalitarians have often supported their case with the conviction that equalization is, as Tawney put it, "one means to a much needed improvement in human relations." He believes that inequality leads to "organized misunderstanding," and "enfeebles, if it does not destroy, the common philosophy required for democracy."[22] Marx, according to

---

[21]*Equality* (London: Allen & Unwin, 1964), pp. 138–40.
[22]Ibid., pp. 33, 264.

Bronfenbrenner, believed that "equality was important only insofar as it might alleviate psychological alienation."[23] T. V. Smith argues similarly that "equality is desirable because it conditions cooperation, that some measure of cooperation is prerequisite to any human life at all, and that a maximum of cooperation is the sine qua non of that good life to which the social prophets and spiritual seers of mankind have long pointed the way."[24]

It is, of course, a basic Marxian insight that difference in economic position is a necessary, but, according to some interpretations, not a sufficient, condition of class consciousness and organized class action. Some egalitarians have argued that reduction of economic inequality is necessary to prevent Marx's prediction of class warfare from coming true. This line of argument, which proceeds from fear, should be distinguished from arguments that emphasize positive gains or that arise from altruistic motives.

In response to this kind of thinking we find counterpropositions by sociologists and social psychologists and others. The consequential argument against equalization is rather involved and has two separate parts. One deals with personal adjustment. Equalization may be taken to mean equalizing opportunity to achieve similar goals. To the extent that people hold similar elevated goals the probability of failure is high. A widespread belief in equality of opportunity heightens the subjective experience of failure and makes personal adjustment more difficult.[25] Those who seek to equalize opportunity may thus contribute to increasing unhappiness, a proposition which would have intrigued Jeremy Bentham. Personal adjustment to the realities of individual differences and social needs will be furthered by establishing a set of differing, meaningful, and reasonably attainable goals, each of which carries status.[26] This prediction has been given wide currency by social psychologists of the Durkheim-Mayo school, as well as by many others.

---

[23]Bronfenbrenner, "Radical Economics in America," pp. 756–57.

[24]*American Philosophy of Equality,* p. ix. As regards political equality, Thomson concludes: "The ultimate and indeed the original reason for political equality . . . is the practical, hard-headed, and realistic one that it works best" (*Equality,* p. 69).

[25]Some observers have attributed recent urban riots by young blacks to undue emphasis upon arbitrary limits to opportunity. They assert that the riots followed disillusionment with the idea that achievement would automatically flow from striking down certain legal barriers.

[26]It is probably true that some of the classical economists explicitly rejected a status society because they thought open competition produced better men. Stigler concludes that "their [the classical economists'] concern was with the maximizing and not with the output. The struggle of men for larger incomes

The second part of the proposition starts from a different point, namely the need of a complex society for differentiation of function. Social differentiation in turn gives rise to and requires differences in world outlook and goals. These differences in world outlook, which some sociologists identify as the essence of class differences,[27] have significance, then, for the workings of a complex society. The family unit transmits these outlook differences in such a way as to handicap children differentially in competition for status, but this means that people are motivated in different directions, which is necessary. If every boy were really striving to become President, and none were aiming at any other goal, a complex and interdependent society would not be possible. Classes, then, are seen as playing the important role of mediating social needs and family and individual goals.

This social-psychological explanation of the beneficial consequences of inequality, which is reminiscent of earlier and conservative writers such as Burke and Maine, must be recorded here as having had a great impact upon the contemporary generation of social scientists. We may conclude that the writing on this proposition has shifted the burden of proof somewhat toward the egalitarians.

Let us pause here to summarize the discussion of consequential propositions. In the discussion of the egalitarian question on the value-judgment level it was concluded that the egalitarian position has made great gains, not only popularly, but among social scientists as well. On the consequential level no such clear conclusion can be reached. As regards the first of the five propositions examined, the utilitarian proposition, the egalitarians have suffered a defeat in seeing it pushed back onto the value-judgment level. On the proposition of equalizing the power-to-decide, the decline of interest in distributivist reform represents a real defeat for egalitarianism. On the other hand, egalitarians may well take comfort from the fact that the proposition relating income inequality to economic progress and efficiency has been severely shaken. More pronouncedly, egalitarians have carried the day on the consequential proposition concerning cultural progress. Finally, with regard to the proposition that economic inequality is necessary to the working of a

---

was good because in the process they learned independence, self-reliance, because in short, they became better men" ("Economists and Equality," p. 4). John Stuart Mill was certainly thinking along these lines when he argued that "as great a demand should be made upon their [all people's] intelligence and virtue as it is in any respect equal to" (*Principles of Political Economy* [New York: D. Appleton & Co., 1909], Book V, Chap. XI, p. 949).

[27]The "culture of poverty" concept, referred to below, is an example of this type of classification.

complex society, egalitarians seem to be on the defensive. Which way the balance has moved among the whole group of five propositions is, of course, very difficult to assess. It is plausible to suggest that there is more agreement, or a narrower area of disagreement, on the consequential level than used to be the case. Points of emphasis have changed, and the burden of proof has been shifted in such a way as to modify and weaken the more "convincing" arguments on both sides.

A further change may be noted from the not too distant past. While once the battle of ideas on the consequential level was a very uneven matter, with all the "respectable" people on one side and only the "underground" willing to carry the flag for lessening of inequality, that is no longer the case. No longer do social scientists approach the subject of inequality as "a region haunted [by] . . . doleful voices and rushings to and fro," as Tawney described it. The consequences of economic inequality and of equalization measures are now the subject of not only speculation but considerable empirical inquiry as well.

THE CAUSES OF ECONOMIC INEQUALITY

Quite distinct from consequential argument is explanation of the causes of an existing pattern of economic inequality[28] and of changes in that pattern. Just as was true of consequential propositions, causation arguments may be approached in a completely objective mood without reference to promotion or discouragement of the egalitarian position on policy matters. However, causation statements do have their policy-influencing significance, through molding of opinion concerning the possibility of actually narrowing inequality. One's view of the causes of poverty is quite likely to influence his attitude toward policies to reduce poverty.

With this in mind we may note a general egalitarian and anti-egalitarian division as regards ideas on the causes of economic inequality. The historic egalitarian position is that inequality is largely or significantly caused by man-made arrangements and socially determined attitudes. This means that the degree of inequality is manipulable within wide ranges. Further, the egalitarian starts off with the suspicion that much inequality is unnecessary.

On the other hand, the anti-egalitarian position is that the causes of

---

[28]For a valuable review of thought on this topic, see Josef J. Spengler, "Hierarchy v. Equality: Persisting Conflict," *Kyklos: International Review for Social Science* 21 (1968), 217–38.

inequality are more basic than a particular set of man-made institutions and attitudes. The causes are believed to be in natural differences among people or in universal social demands. Hence the pattern and degree of inequality are not manipulable, or at any rate, not easily so. The Marxian association of increasing inequality with capitalism is perhaps a halfway house between what we have called the egalitarian and anti-egalitarian emphases.

Once we have stated this general division of opinion, it must next be noted that discussion on the causation level is highly unorganized. There are few propositions on which debate is joined. The shelves are stacked with a great variety of causation statements, many of them untested, some untestable, and only a few the subject of lively controversy.

Numerous statements are easily accepted as plausible partial explanations of economic inequality even though it is difficult to assess their quantitative significance. Thus on the egalitarian side, arguments which are entered without objection include the following. Inequality is caused by attitudes toward it. Tawney emphasized what he called a "religion of inequality," which involves a "tranquil inhumanity on the part of the rich and a passive acceptance by the poor." De Jouvenel, though not an egalitarian, offers the insight that it is not the strong oppressing the weak which is characteristic of inequality, but that unequal positions are willingly accorded those who are generally admired and believed to be superior.[29]

Another egalitarian proposition is that an original pattern of inequality may be rigidified through institutional arrangements which perpetuate inequalities of opportunity. Laws of inheritance are only one example. Others are the practice of nepotism, class favoritism, discrimination on grounds of race, sex, and age, restriction of educational opportunity, unequal distribution of sanitation and health protection.

On the anti-egalitarian side some propositions have been put forth with little objection. One is that there is at least a historical association between economic inequality and size of the social unit. Similarly, inequality is associated with the degree of specialization of functions, the pattern of ownership of physical and human capital, the rate of economic change or progress, and basic social characteristics.

In contrast to the above propositions, which have encountered little objection, there are some which have been the subject of considerable

---

[29]*Ethics of Redistribution,* pp. 78–81. Veblen also wrote in a similar vein. For this same insight into the causes of inequality see Mark Twain's *A Connecticut Yankee in King Arthur's Court.*

controversy. Two are worth special attention: (1) the proposition that the causes of inequality are such that the pattern of income inequality is virtually the same in all times and places; and (2) the proposition that income inequality arises out of differences in personal abilities to perform necessary tasks.

Protagonists on both sides of the egalitarian question have appealed to the "naturalness" of some stated pattern of inequality. In 1754 Rousseau asserted that a pattern of rough equality obtained in the "natural" social arrangement. Many responses to Rousseau's assumption have been forthcoming, intending to document the original and universal reality of inequality. Leading among these responses is the famous Pareto Law, which was based on the finding of a striking similarity in the distribution of upper incomes in widely differing settings.

It is probably fair to conclude that recent inquiries into comparative income distribution have unsettled the Pareto Law considerably. There is, however, widespread agreement that the range of inequality which it is possible to find is not so wide as some egalitarians seem to have suggested. Studies comparing inequality in the Soviet Union with inequality in capitalist nations would seem to invalidate the easy association sometimes drawn between capitalism and inequality.

An egalitarian proposition sometimes offered is that income inequality cannot be caused solely by individuals' differing abilities because abilities seem to be distributed along a normal curve while incomes are highly skewed in distribution.[30] D. G. Champernowne offers the interesting insight that a skewed distribution of income will arise and persist out of a series of random shocks to an original equal distribution of income.[31] Others argue that while it is true that the distribution of some particular abilities, such as those measured by the Stanford-Binet test, approximate a normal curve; the distributions of other particular abilities, of which the ability to earn income may be one, approximate the skewness of the actual income distribution. It is important to recognize that *combinations* of abilities are required in some performance tests. Some writers on poverty emphasize combinations of *disabilities* in explaining skewness of the income curve at the low end. Gary S. Becker explains skewness by the positive correlation between ability and "investment in human capital." He argues that those with higher ability receive higher rates of return and thus have more incentive to invest in

---

[30]For a review of some of the literature on this, see Jacob Mincer, "The Distribution of Labor Incomes: A Survey with Special Reference to the Human Capital Approach," *Journal of Economic Literature* 8 (March 1970), 1–26.

[31]"A Model of Income Distribution," *Economic Journal* 63 (1953).

education.[32] Stanley Lebergott explains skewness as the result of quite rational inequality in the supply of credit to individuals.[33] This would suggest, then, that inequalities of income may be explained by the nature of the "games" for which rewards are payable in society as related to the distribution of special abilities to perform at those "games." Further, it has been suggested by Milton Friedman that the degree of inequality is influenced by the general distribution of willingness to take chances for large gains as contrasted with desire for smaller though more certain incomes.[34]

It is possible for a disinterested observer to conclude that there has been a narrowing of disagreement on the causation level. The egalitarians have gained recognition of the fact that the causes of economic inequality are such that the pattern is, at least to some extent, variable and manipulable. On the other hand, the anti-egalitarians have retained the notion that some part of existing inequality arises from deep-seated social needs and basic differences among people.

The theory of the causation of inequality must have in it an explanation of how those who are poorest were selected for that status. Three possible theories, which overlap to some degree, can be considered as having some merit. (1) Events, which are random in their incidence, select people for poverty status. (2) social barriers of class and caste and custom provide a basis for selection of people for this status and work to reinforce this selection by differential provision of economic opportunities. (3) Personal differences of ability and motivation, either inherent or acquired, function to select candidates for poverty status.

The first of these theories would focus attention on the things which happen to individuals—on the risks which we all run. There is the risk of being born poor, the risk of disability or premature death of the family breadwinner, the risk of family breakup, the risk of outliving one's savings in old age. There is the risk of business failure, of decline of status for one's chosen occupation, industry, or region. Events which yield differential chances to be rich or poor are happening at any moment in time and these differences, to a certain extent at least, can be considered to be beyond the control of the individual. The importance of

---

[32]*Human Capital: A Theoretical and Empirical Analysis with Special Reference to Education* (New York: National Bureau of Economic Research, 1964).

[33]"The Shape of the Income Distribution," *American Economic Review* 49 (June 1959), 328–47.

[34]"Choice, Chance and the Personal Distribution of Income," *Journal of Political Economy* 61 (August 1953), 277–90.

these events is seen in the high incidence of poverty among the aged, disabled, women, farmers, and unemployed.

The social-barriers theory urges the idea that society deliberately, although perhaps not consciously nor explicitly, selects people to be poor and by formal and informal policy makes it difficult for them to escape from poverty. The clearest example of this type of policy in this country is racial discrimination, but there are other types of discrimination and segregation. Some of these barriers alienate the poor from the general community and encourage them to adopt an ethic which is sometimes called a "culture of poverty" and which is hostile to escape from poverty. This means that the poor build their own barriers in some cases.

The personal differences theory would suggest that some would and some would not be thrown into or kept in poverty by a certain set of events or by particular barriers. We know that some individuals overcome great handicaps to emerge from poverty. Here we confront the age-old question whether heredity or environment is more important in determining success and failure. And we cannot avoid the question of free will versus determinism. Data concerning innate as opposed to acquired characteristics of the poor and nonpoor are very limited and it is difficult to separate cause from consequence. For example, we know that the poor tend to have less education and more illness than the nonpoor, but it is not entirely clear which way the causation runs.

We said that each of these theories has some merit. That is, each one explains some of the poverty which is found in the United States today. The diversity of causes suggests that a diversity of remedies may be needed.

THE DETERMINANTS OF EGALITARIANISM

Why are some individuals or groups predisposed to favor or oppose economic equalization? Many writers have expressed doubt that inquiries on the consequential and causation levels are determinative of the position taken on the value-judgment level.[35] Further explanation is

---

[35]This doubt is strengthened by the fact that equalization measures are sometimes enacted or proposed first and consequential arguments supporting those measures are developed later. Thus Blum and Kalven note that it is difficult to trace a connection between the intellectual justifications of progressive taxation and the adoption of such legislation. "Certainly the most rigorous analysis of progression came only after the idea had become a political reality" (*Uneasy Case*, p. 14).

sought in the motives and circumstances of the protagonists. At this level of discussion, then, we stand completely aside from the merits of the arguments reviewed above and adopt the belief, with Lecky, that "men are chiefly persuaded, not by the logical force of arguments, but by the disposition with which they view them."

Several varieties of speculative statement may be noted. One variety has to do with personal motives. Egalitarians have, on occasion, attributed selfish motives to those who have opposed equalization. The first or virgin stage of an egalitarian movement may be marked as that in which its antagonists are seen as having only selfish motives, while the egalitarians are thought of as free from economic interest.[36] On the other hand, it is common practice to derogate the egalitarian position as an expression of envy. Thus Oliver Wendell Holmes wrote to Harold Laski, "I have no respect for the passion for equality, which seems to me merely idealizing envy. . . ." Brand Whitlock caustically identified a reformer as one who feels "a deep and abiding responsibility for the shortcomings of others." Still thinking along the lines of personal reactions, some writers have emphasized that we do not resent the economic success of those of whom we approve as individuals. Neither do we feel badly about the economic failure of those of whom we disapprove, or with whom we share no sense of community. It is ironic that a person may simultaneously register bitterness toward the lack of sharing by those above him in status ranking, and feel no obligation to share with those who rank below him.[37] This suggests that egalitarian positions are adopted purely and simply out of self-interest. In this view, a richer person will sacrifice for the poorer only if he feels threatened if he does not do so.[38]

It is alleged that spokesmen for equality really want some kind of social change other than economic equalization. Holmes divined that "some kind of despotism is at the bottom of the seeking for change." De Jouvenel sees the contemporary situation in Western democracies as one "in which the egalitarian ideal is put to work in all good faith, for ends other than itself," namely a switch over to a new leadership and

---

[36]Vernon L. Parrington in his *Main Currents in American Thought* (New York: Harcourt, Brace, 1930), referred to Western egalitarians as "agrarian democrats" but to Eastern conservatives as "economic interest" groups.

[37]Ludwig von Mises observes that when the American worker sloganizes about equality he does not have in mind sharing his income with the two-thirds of the world's population who have less income than he has.

[38]See Kenneth E. Boulding's interesting essay on threats and altruism as motives for philanthropy, "The Grants Economy" (Michigan Economic Association, March 22, 1968), esp. pp. 127–28.

class pattern. Daniel P. Moynihan detects a "proclivity for seeing in the poor and dispossessed—however weak and outnumbered they may be—an instrument for transforming the larger society."[39] Other writers, notably Schumpeter, have suggested that intellectuals, including social scientists, are likely to evaluate a social arrangement with reference to the status it accords them. Hence it may be that some who now advocate equalization would not do so if they were accorded more recognition within the present framework. Disaffected members of an elite are most likely to be "inequality conscious" and to adopt egalitarianism as an engine to power for themselves.

Proceeding now toward slightly more high-flown theories of egalitarianism, we come to the proposition that as inequality is abated, the demand for further equalization increases. Thus equalization feeds upon itself, as was noted by de Tocqueville:

> The hatred that men bear to privilege increases in proportion as privileges become fewer and less considerable, so that democratic passions would seem to burn most fiercely just when they have least fuel. . . . When all conditions are unequal, no inequality is so great as to offend the eye, whereas the least dissimilarity is odious in the midst of general uniformity; the more complete this uniformity is, the more insupportable the sight of such a difference becomes. Hence it is natural that love of equality should constantly increase together with the equality itself, and that it should grow by what it feeds on.[40]

T. H. Marshall emphasizes the idea that a free contract society opens the way for direct comparison of all people in a society against the yardstick of a single standard of living, thus encouraging invidious comparison. As soon as a society has one "way of life" rather than many, inequality becomes less tolerable. He points out that in the modern economy, "The working classes, instead of inheriting a distinctive though simple culture, are provided with a cheap and shoddy imitation of a civilization that has become national."[41]

---

[39]"The Professors and the Poor," p. 28.

[40]*Democracy in America*, II, 295.

[41]*Citizenship and Social Class* (Cambridge, England: Cambridge University Press, 1949), pp. 30–31. Marshall observes that "social integration spread from the sphere of sentiment and patriotism into that of material enjoyment. The components of a civilized and cultural life, formerly the monopoly of the few, were brought progressively within the reach of the many, who were thereby encouraged to stretch out their hands toward those that still eluded their grasp. The diminution of inequality strengthened the demand for its abolition, at least with regard to the essentials of social welfare" (p. 47).

Corollary to this is the idea that egalitarianism is related to the absolute level of living. The poor ordinarily are not agitators for equalization. As Hugh Dalton observed, "It is the patience of the poor that most strikes those who know them." He concludes:

> Only when men have a surplus of energy over and above that necessary for earning a living, have they the time, or the power or the spirit to take stock of their conditions and to ponder large projects of improvement.[42]

David Potter explains the American "national character" by our exceptional economic success.

> Abundance has influenced American life in many ways, but there is perhaps no respect in which the influence has been more profound than in the forming and strengthening of the American ideal and practice of equality, with all that the ideal has implied for the individual in the way of opportunity to make his own place in society and of emancipation from a system of status.[43]

Egalitarian argument is causally associated with groups which have experienced significant changes in relative economic and social position.[44] Crane Brinton offers a historical generalization.

> In general the demand for equality has flared up strongly only when there was a marked contrast between the customary status of a group or groups of men and their actual status. The French Revolution is here the *locus classicus:* the middle classes were

---

[42]*Some Aspects of the Inequality of Incomes in Modern Communities* (rev. ed.; London: Routledge & Sons, 1925), p. 5. Compare Arnold J. Toynbee, *Civilization on Trial* (New York: Oxford University Press, 1948), p. 26.

[43]*People of Plenty* (Chicago: University of Chicago Press, 1954), p. 91.

[44]Engels concluded that "the idea of equality, . . . both in its bourgeois and in its proletarian form, is itself a historical product, the creation of which required definite historical conditions which in turn themselves presuppose a long previous historical development. It is therefore anything but an eternal truth" (*Anti-Dühring* [New York: International Publishers, 1939], p. 118; see chap. 10, which considers this subject). It is not altogether clear what the causal sequence looked like to Engels. Proletarian demands for equality, which are by definition "demands for the abolition of classes," are (1) spontaneous, (2) taught to them by the bourgeoisie, (3) due to the general diffusion of the idea, and (4) due to "the continued appropriateness of the idea."

Many writers have emphasized the class basis of egalitarianism. Thus Élie Halévy finds the aim of Benthamism was "to develop the middle class: to this can be reduced the equalitarianism of Bentham and James Mill" (*The Growth of Philosophic Radicalism* [London: Faber & Faber, 1952], p. 366).

as rich and as well educated as the nobility but were in a position of definite social and legal inferiority.[45]

A more inclusive theory would include the idea that when a superior group's economic status is falling, we would expect to hear a denial of the value of economic equality and perhaps (depending on the existing distribution of rights) the appeal to some other variety, such as political or legal or religious equality. Political responsibility may make a difference, since equality as a group claim to be made good against foreign and opposing groups is one matter, equality as an operating principle within the group quite another.

Egalitarian argument has served many masters as it has ricocheted through modern history from country to country, from class to class. It is noteworthy that much, if not most, such argument has been advanced by or on behalf of groups other than the poor. Thus we find the championship of equality passing from the British and French to the Americans to the colonial and "developing" national economies, from the bourgeoisie to the proletarians, from whites to nonwhites, with each group furnishing ideological ammunition to its successors. History provides numerous examples of the arguments for equality as formulated by one person or group anomalously serving as a rationale for the policies of another.

We have noted that egalitarianism has been explained by reference to personal motives of selfishness or envy or malice, the latter being directed toward certain sets of unequals. It may also be explained by prior changes in absolute and relative standards of living, and by shifts in class and group status.

Some part of the success of egalitarianism must be set down to the overstatement of consequential argument by the opponents of particular equalization measures. When opposition is rallied by the prediction of dire consequences which do not clearly materialize, it is difficult to gather political defenses against succeeding measures by the use of the previously losing argument.[46]

---

[45]"Equality," *Encyclopedia of Social Sciences,* Vol. 5, p. 580. (His example suggests that by "actual status" he means a recently acquired status.) The contrast between educational attainment and income of young adult Negroes in the United States provides a case in point. Median years of schooling is about the same for younger whites and blacks, yet earnings are substantially lower for blacks at each educational level.

[46]J. K. Galbraith, *Economics and the Art of Controversy* (New Brunswick, N.J.: Rutgers University Press, 1955), pp. 75–92. "One of the most surprising features of social welfare legislation is its inability to sustain controversy once it has passed into law" (ibid., p. 80).

A complete theory must set out the conditions for decline as well as for success of economic egalitarianism. Recent effort to narrow inequality is largely the spelling out of old policies and older ideas. Egalitarian thought as applied to economic affairs has proceeded largely on the basis of a few great affirmative rushes of the previous century. Egalitarianism has advanced on a moving front and has been transmuted from a generalized set of formal doctrines into a set of particular programs for practical equalization in economic affairs. However, throughout the long process of interaction between doctrine and practice it has become clear that the economists who have sponsored egalitarianism have been interested in both more and less than economic equality. They have been interested in less than economic equality in the sense that they do not seek the elimination of all existing economic inequalities, but only those which are seen to be "arbitrary," "capricious," or "functionless." They have been interested in more than equality in the sense that they hold economic equalization only as a proximate or conditional goal.[47] With all the move from general to specific content of egalitarianism, the spirit of egalitarianism is elusive. Interest in economic equalization is undoubtedly at least partly based on the hope of a more spiritual relationship among people, a "parity of esteem" which is not simply a lack of class feeling but "a positive feeling of respect for all engaged in a common purpose."[48]

The process of equalization and poverty reduction has been powered by deeply rooted doctrine and energized by successful experiment. It may be that interest in further economic equalization will flag only as there is widespread adoption of the view that the "something less" than equality has been accomplished and only as we come to believe that existing inequalities are necessary and functional, or at least not destructive or oppressive. Finally, that interest may diminish if people come to believe that further equalization will lead away from rather than toward the "something more" than equality, namely feelings of fraternity and mutual respect.

---

[47]Most spokesmen for egalitarianism would agree with Stigler that "rule of thumb guides such as greater equality . . . are insufficient to distinguish policies that lead to very different types of society, and therefore to distinguish good from bad policies" ("Economists and Equality," p. 8).

[48]Samuel H. Beer, "Fabianism Revisited" (symposium by Seymour Harris and others), *Review of Economics and Statistics* 35 (August 1953), 206.

Chapter 3

DEVELOPMENT OF A SPECIFIC POVERTY-REDUCTION GOAL

In chapter 1 we reviewed the historical record of popular interest in poverty and of antipoverty efforts. In chapter 2 we reviewed social science thought on the broad topic of inequality, of which poverty is a subtopic. Both chapters indicate that any of a wide range of interpretations and emphases is possible for public policy under the heading of concern for the poor and lessening of inequality. Clearly, a long leap is required to get from such broad considerations to a statement of objectives for the poor. In this chapter we seek further understanding of the way in which the goal of poverty reduction as it has been stated, and as I would further modify that statement, relates to the facts and issues of inequality. The goal may be said to derive from a general concern with inequality and a more specific concern with *income* inequality. Attention is shifted from overall sharing of income to more specific inquiry into the conditions of living of those at the low end of the income scale, and to identification of "the poor." The goal is stated as the elimination of income poverty, which means bringing all persons above selected income lines. This requires the adoption of ways to measure progress toward the goal. A further refinement (and one that I recommend) is to state, as part of the goal, a specific timetable for the reduction of income poverty.[1]

Looking at the percentage of people below an arbitrarily set poverty line differs from two other, more traditional, methods of appraising income distribution. One method is to look to the functional shares of income, i.e., the division of income between labor and property. A second method is to examine the size distribution of income with all income-receiving units ranked from richest to poorest in terms of total money (or money plus nonmoney) income. Inequality in the size distribution is commonly expressed in terms of the share of all income going to the top 10 percent and each other 10 percent of income receivers.

---

[1]We should note here that neither President Johnson nor President Nixon has stated any such timetable. Also, we do not want the reader to be misled into thinking that what follows is a historical account of decisions taken in the period when the Economic Opportunity Act was under consideration.

FUNCTIONAL DISTRIBUTION OF INCOME

The use of the gross national product of the American economy, which in 1967 was running at the rate of $790 billion, is divided among consumers, governments, and business firms on the basis of 65, 20, and 15 percent for each, respectively. The division is effected by purchases, which are made out of the incomes of households and business firms and the tax revenues of governments. These purchases in turn give rise to incomes, thus making a circular flow. Incomes take the form of labor income, property income, and transfer payments. (The latter are payments made on a basis other than for current production.) Of income payments for current production, about 75 percent are for labor and 25 percent are for use of property. About 6 percent of these income payments are transferred by governments from one set of businesses and households to another. Further transfers are accomplished privately.

An individual, if he is to survive, must either earn income or tie into a public or private transferring institution. It is a corollary of this that an individual will have a low income if he supplies little salable labor or property service and if he has only a limited claim on the secondary distribution.

The three-fourths of the national income which goes to labor includes some income to self-employed farmers, businessmen, and professionals, but the larger part goes to employees, who make up 80 percent of the labor force. There is, of course, considerable inequality in the distribution of labor income.

Property income consists of profits, interest, and rent. The largest part of this is profit. Corporation profits take 10 percent of national income, and a similar share goes to profits of unincorporated enterprises. Interest and rent combined amount to only 5 percent of the national income. These incomes from "passive ownership" amount to a smaller total than is redistributed in the form of "welfare state" benefits, to which we will return shortly.

Property income, aside from the rent of land, arises out of the accumulated capital invested in business enterprises and residential structures. The aggregate value of all producer wealth in the nation (excluding automobiles and other consumer durables) now approaches $2 trillion and yields about $150 billion of income. Personal and corporate savings add to the national business wealth at the rate of $90 billion a year, thus contributing to the future productivity of labor as well as to future amounts of property income.

Property income, most notably profit, and the wealth which gives rise to it, is much more unequal in its distribution than is labor income.

It is true that certain types of property such as homes (60 percent of American families own their own homes) and life insurance policies are widely distributed. And it is true that 12 percent of families own some stock in business corporations, and that millions more indirectly own business securities through insurance and bank deposits and private pension rights. However, wealth remains highly concentrated—with the top 10 percent of families, ranked by wealth, holding over 50 percent of the total and the lowest one-third holding only 1 percent. The top 1 percent hold three-fourths of the corporate stock. While there is far less wealth inequality than in England, we should not be blinded to the fact that most Americans still own little wealth, and most of them do not have direct title to any business wealth in the form of stocks, bonds, or equity in a farm or business. For most families, income-earning power is largely restricted to the labor power of family members and to the home they own. In 1962 the median net worth of all spending units was found to be $7550. For those spending units with incomes under $3000, the median net worth was $2760.[2]

The principal distinction in functional income distribution is that between income to labor and income to property. However, another type of income is governmental transfer payments, which do not arise in the process of production but rather are financed out of taxes. These transfers, which include relief, or assistance, and social insurance payments (e.g., unemployment compensation and old age insurance), currently amount to more than 6 percent of national income.

Over time, labor income and public transfer payments have become relatively more important as types of income. Self-employment has declined and government employment has increased. Simultaneously, the extended family has become less important as a redistributor of income. It can be argued that increased reliance upon labor income and the breakdown of the extended family have given rise to new problems of income insecurity and irregularity which have called forth new arrangements for public redistribution. The problems of income management no doubt influence private decisions about family formation, responsibility for relatives, labor-force participation by secondary earners, savings, insurance, and provisions for extraordinary needs at various stages in the life cycle. Hence it may be that private redistribution of income is changing over time in such a way as to offset the apparent equalizing effect of the rise in public transfers.

---

[2] *Federal Reserve Bulletin* (March 1964). See also the *Survey of Financial Characteristics of Consumers,* Board of Governors of the Federal Reserve System (1966).

SIZE DISTRIBUTION OF INCOME

This brings us to the second method of appraising income distribution, which is to rank personally received incomes by size and to determine how income is shared among those with relatively high and low incomes. In the United States in recent years, the top 10 percent of income receivers has received about 28 percent of total money income and the lowest 10 percent about 2 percent of income. The share of the lowest 20 percent of income receivers has been about 5 percent of total money income.[3]

This degree of inequality is about midway between the relatively egalitarian patterns of the Netherlands and the Scandinavian countries on the one hand, and the more unequal distributions of, say, Italy and Ceylon on the other. It is generally believed by experts in this field that income is more unequally distributed in the less-developed countries than it is in the contemporary United States. However, this comparison is difficult to make because of differences in economic and social structure and in the forms that income payment and income sharing may take. Perhaps it is for this reason that the Soviet Union and other communist nations have declined to publish size-distribution data. Similarly, time-series data on size distribution are hard to analyze because what is comprehended in the key definitions of income, income period, and income-receiving unit changes over time. Careful working and reworking of all available data by numerous scholars have produced a consensus that there was indeed a lessening of inequality in the United States during 1938–48 and no clear trend one way or another during 1948–67. The lessening of inequality seems to have been confined to those groups within the top half of the income distribution, with no great change in the income share of, and no change in inequality within, the bottom half. The lowest fifth of families received 5.0 percent of "total money income" in 1947 and 5.4 percent in 1967 (see Table 3.1). Edward C. Budd concludes, after a careful study of all available data, that the postwar years have seen a slight gain in share of income by the families in the fortieth to ninety-fourth percentiles, at the expense of the bottom forty and the top six percentiles.[4]

However, as we noted earlier, so many variables come into the picture that one must be wary of any easy generalizations. For example,

---

[3]This particular pattern of sharing is the result of numerous patterns within different groups. For example, inequality among nonwhites is greater than among whites, and inequality among the old is greater than among the young.

[4]"Postwar Changes in the Size Distribution of Income in the United States," American Economic Association, *Proceedings* 60 (May 1970), 247–60.

Table 3.1.   Shares of Total Money Income, by Fifths of Families
(Selected Years)

Percent distribution of aggregate income	1947[a]	1949[b]	1959[b]	1964[b]	1967[a]
Lowest fifth	5.0	4.5	5.1	5.2	5.4
2	11.8	11.9	12.1	12.0	12.2
3	17.0	17.3	17.8	17.6	17.5
4	23.1	23.5	23.6	24.0	23.7
Highest fifth	43.0	42.8	41.4	41.1	41.2
Top 5 percent	17.2	16.9	16.3	15.4	15.3

[a]Source: U.S. Bureau of the Census, *Income in 1967 of Families in the U.S.*, Current Population Reports, Consumer Income, Ser. P–60, No. 59 (April 18, 1969), Table 5, p. 24.

[b]Source: U.S. Bureau of the Census, *Trends in the Income of Families and Persons in the U.S., 1947–1964*, Technical Paper No. 17 (Washington, D.C.: Government Printing Office, 1967), Table 33, pp. 215–17.

family size moved into closer positive association with level of income. There was undoubling (for example, aged parents moving into separate housing) of middle- and lower-income families, earlier marriage, and a rise in number of children for upper-income families, thus suggesting that the decline in inequality is understated by a simple consumer-unit distribution. However, home-produced goods and services (which are relatively more important to the poor) fell in importance, and capital gains and expense-account living (more important for the rich) increased —suggesting that the decline in inequality is overstated by accounting only for money income.[5]

There has been a stability in the overall distribution of wealth[6] and income which is remarkable in view of the great changes which have occurred in the economic structure and in income and wealth levels. The Marxian predictions both of inevitably increasing immiseration of the masses and of increasing concentration of wealth under capitalism have been proved completely wrong by American experience.

It would have been possible tor President Johnson to state an anti-poverty goal in terms of either the functional or the size distribution of income.[7] Thus he could have called for an increase in the labor share

[5]Robert J. Lampman, "Recent Changes in Income Inequality Reconsidered," *American Economic Review* 44 (June 1954), 251–68.

[6]Robert J. Lampman, *The Share of Top Wealth-Holders in National Wealth, 1922–1956* (Princeton, N.J.: Princeton University Press for the National Bureau of Economic Research, 1962).

[7]To think on a quite different track, he could have said the goal is to increase the share of national income going to nonwhites.

of national income, or for a more widespread ownership of wealth.[8] Alternatively, he might have set forth the goal in terms of the share of income going to the bottom fifth.[9] Thus he could have said the goal is to increase their share from 5 to 6 percent of total income. Such a goal would have suffered from the fact that size-distribution data do not standardize for the nature of the income-receiving units. In other words, they do not adjust for the fact that large and small families are lumped together in the rankings. Poverty lines can adjust for family size and hence indicate more about levels of living than do standard size distributions of income.

THE GOAL OF POVERTY REDUCTION

Instead of turning the nation's attention to either the functional or the size distribution of income, advisers to the President looked to level-of-living distinctions and suggested the goal of "eliminating poverty." It seems fair to say that human interest in income distribution progressively rises as we shift attention from functional shares, through size distribution, to the poverty-line or level-of-living distinctions. This is a shift from the concern with Ricardian factors of production and Marxian abstract masses in the grip of abstract forces, to concern with ordinary people in trouble. Between 1947 and 1960 unattached individuals, the aged, female heads, and not-in-labor-force heads increased in the bottom fifth. This led some to observe that low income was not so much the product of class or economic problems as a sign of social or political failure. The fact that the low-income group included so many who were without influence or even without families and who were out of the mainstream of the economy made the inequality *seem* different even if it was not quantitatively very different.

It needs to be underlined that the poverty line, as drawn by the Johnson administration and continued in use by the Nixon administration, is not simply a line through the size distribution of income. It is a series of lines, one for each family size, and with a difference for farm as

---

[8]A way to pursue the latter goal is suggested by Louis O. Kelso and Patricia Hetter in *Two-Factor Theory: The Economics of Reality* (New York: Vintage Books, 1968).

[9]There are various ways to state such a goal. One is to set a poverty line not in static dollar terms, but as a moving line. For example, one could say the goal is to bring families over a poverty line defined as that income equal to one-half the median income. According to the latter measure, there has been virtually no poverty reduction (see S. M. Miller and Pamela Roby, *The Future of Inequality* [New York: Basic Books, 1970]).

opposed to nonfarm residence.[10] And, as we stated earlier, the goal is to reduce the number of families below those lines. Stating the goal this way is to declare a national minimum—an income level for each family size below which we do not want any American to have to live. A second part of the goal is to cut the size of the poverty-income gap.

NOVELTY OF THIS GOAL

That two-part goal is a nova in the constellation of purposes which guide our national efforts. Or, to switch metaphorical horses, it is a rather specialized branch of a tree of goals whose roots are embedded in concern with the individual's freedom and security, his opportunities and responsibilities, his right to privacy, and his duty to participate. These goals, and government's role in pursuing them, have changed over time in response to shifts in the economic and social environment and with new insights concerning what is feasible in social affairs.

The decision to pursue the reduction of poverty would seem to follow naturally enough out of a long train of extensions of citizenship and a gradual conversion from thinking of the poor as a hostile force, to be isolated and contained, to the vision of them as full members of a democratic society, whose fate is linked with that of the general community and who therefore are worth investing in as latent assets to the community. The decision to adopt an antipoverty goal may also be said to flow from earlier decisions concerning such closely related policies as assuring security against income loss, facilitating collective bargaining, and promoting full employment and economic growth.

The way our goals evolve contributes to their overlapping character. Often one goal has been implicit in earlier ones. Hence one could argue that declaring economic growth a goal is merely a new rationalization for policies which had already been justified on other grounds. Similarly, the antipoverty goal offers a new reason for interest in the goals of full employment, economic growth, and equality of opportunity.[11] Thus,

---

[10]Originally, the Council of Economic Advisers set only two lines, one for families and one for unrelated individuals. Further adjustments were introduced in testimony on the Economic Opportunity Act. The specific lines now in use were spelled out by Mollie Orshansky in the *Social Security Bulletin* (January 1965, pp. 5–11, and July 1965, pp. 3–10). They were later adopted by the Office of Economic Opportunity.

[11]Cf. Robert J. Lampman, "Recent U.S. Economic Growth and the Gain in Human Welfare," in Walter W. Heller, ed., *Perspectives on Economic Growth* (New York: Random House, 1969), pp. 143–62.

making the elimination of poverty an explicit goal is to refresh and reinvigorate earlier commitments.

But it is more than a restatement. It carries with it a challenge to some established purposes and policies; it puts a sharper edge on the measurement of the performance of our national economy. It asks not only whether we have high employment, but who is unemployed. It asks not only whether average income is rising, but what is happening to incomes of specific groups. It even asks whether hot and heavy pursuit of the goals of full employment and rapid economic growth is like enriching the diets of all simply because a few are underweight.[12] It asks whether unemployment can be more generously shared by the nonpoor, and whether the poor can participate more directly in measures to promote economic growth. It also involves asking whose incomes are being secured, whose wages and whose prices are being protected, thus raising anew the issue of legitimacy of claims by private parties to government support and protection.

Stating the antipoverty goal implies that poverty is a good basis for discriminating among claimants for public funds or for limiting government participation in economic affairs. Is it possible that we do not have a farm problem or an old-age problem or an urban problem or a housing problem—but that all these are, in essence, insofar as governmental intervention is needed, one and the same poverty problem? Does one who has a certain income or occupational status and then loses it have more claim than one who never had such status? In other words, should protection of income continuity be viewed as more important for government attention than promotion of income adequacy?

An agreed-upon poverty line offers one of many possible guides for income redistribution.[13] It poses an alternative and a challenge to redistribution *from* the poor or the rich *toward* the aged, the sick, the unemployed, the victims of flood or fire, those who live in low-income neighborhoods or regions, those who suffer from racial discrimination, or those in certain occupations. If poverty were eliminated, there would doubtless still be dependency of some on others; some discrimination on grounds of age, sex, and color; and some territorial differences in income. Poverty is not the same thing as dependency, discrimination,

---

[12]This is a rough translation of one of the leading questions raised by John Kenneth Galbraith in *The Affluent Society* (Boston: Houghton Mifflin, 1958). The question's cogency is partly due to the fact that most of today's unemployed are not poor.

[13]It may be objected that it is not a sufficient guide since it fails to specify the group from which income is to be redistributed. Are the near-poor to bear the burden of such policy? Is the cost to be met only by the top fifth of families?

accidental loss, or regional depression, and it is not the inexorable result of them. The point is that redistribution toward the poor is different from redistribution toward other target groups. Hence, in setting the poverty line, a number of considerations should be borne in mind. An important policy judgment is being made.

SETTING THE POVERTY LINES

We have already stated that we equate the antipoverty goal with setting a national minimum income, adjusted for family size. But how is the particular minimum level to be selected in accord with an acceptable notion of poverty? Would it be better if we had somehow been able to avoid the use of the term "poverty" in addressing ourselves to the concerns of those with low incomes? There are several reasons why the latter question has to be answered. One has to do with the relativity of what is thought of as income poverty over time and space. Another reason is that some people deny that poverty has much to do with income. In what follows we argue that there are some reasonable ways of connecting up the use of the complex term "poverty" with the goal of attenuating the low end of the income distribution.

As long ago as 1883, William Graham Sumner objected that there was no possible definition of a "poor man" and that the concept was dangerously elastic. The concept is elastic if we consider poverty to mean relative lack of income, and it is elastic if we think of it as referring to something other than income. Let us review, first, the relativity of "income poverty."

Most of us would agree that poverty relates, at least in part, to a discrepancy between needs and resources—or between needed and actual consumption. The "needs" of people are, of course, hard to specify. They might be set at that level of income necessary to maintain the level of population. By that standard, most of the nations of the world have incomes that average above poverty levels, because their populations are increasing. In this century the world population has already doubled once and may be expected to double again. But the needs of people may also be said to relate to those goods and services above a subsistence level which enable them to live in some dignity and to participate in the social and political life of their country. Hence, poverty is relative to average levels of living which have been attained at a given time and place.

By present-day American standards most of the several billions of people who have ever lived, and most of the three billion people alive today, were or are poor. In 1967 the median family income in America was $8000. Even in 1914 it was relatively high—on the order of $2700 (in dollars of 1967 purchasing power).

Americans, who make up only 6 percent of the world's population, produce and consume over one-third of the world's output of goods and services. Their income level is hence something like five or six times as high as the world's average—or about twice that of Western Europe, at least ten times that of Asia.[14] This income gap has narrowed with reference to some fast-growing economies such as Japan, but for the most part comparative rates of growth in per capita income portend a continuing—and in some cases a widening—gap between our economic attainment and that of most other nations. Only a minority of the people in the world live at much above subsistence levels. In this world picture the United States and a few other advanced nations stand as a mountain range in a swamp of poverty and misery. The striking difference in living standard is highlighted by the fact that the average income of one of the most disadvantaged of American groups, namely Negroes, is above that of Frenchmen and Englishmen.

By any broad comparative standard, then, the typical American worker—and even the typical low-income family—are rich. They are rich because of the productivity of the national economy, and because of the way in which the product is shared. To talk about poverty in America in the late twentieth century is to use the term in a special way.[15]

Dorothy Brady is one of several scholars to point out that there seems to have been a tendency to set poverty lines in such a way that virtually the same proportions of the population are found to be "poor" or below a minimum standard of living in widely varying times and places. This suggests that when poverty, as presently defined, is eliminated in

---

[14]Students of economics will recognize that there is an index number problem in making these comparisons. Prices tend to vary among countries in such a way that the typical American worker cannot buy two or ten times the quantity of the basket goods and services commonly consumed in Europe or Asia. At the same time, foreigners cannot buy as much as one-half or one-tenth of the basket of goods commonly consumed in the United States.

[15]It would follow from this that each country might well have a different poverty line. Recent studies of poverty in other nations include the following: Brian Abel-Smith and Peter Townsend, *The Poor and the Poorest* (London: G. Ball and Sons, Ltd., 1965); Ronald F. Henderson, "The Dimensions of Poverty," *Proceedings* of the 35th Summer School of the Australian Institute of Political Science, Canberra (January 1969); Lee Soltow, "The Magnitude of Low Income Groups in Scandinavia," Discussion Paper 26–68, Institute for Research on Poverty, University of Wisconsin (1968); Koji Taira, "Consumer Preferences, Poverty Norms, and Extent of Poverty," Reprint No. 63, Research Center in Economic Growth, Stanford University (1969).

the United States, another President may start out to eliminate poverty, using another definition, all over again. To keep this in perspective, it should be emphasized that the "tendency to set poverty lines" referred to by Professor Brady has never before been drawn into a national policy effort of the kind started here in 1964. Hence I dismiss as quite irrelevant the scattered, unofficial, and variously purposed "poverty lines" which have been offered at other times and places.[16] While income poverty is a relative matter, I do not think we should engage in frequent changes of the poverty lines, other than to adjust for price change. As I see it, the elimination of income poverty is usefully thought of as a one-time operation in pursuit of a goal unique to this generation. That goal should be achieved before 1980, at which time the next generation will have set new economic and social goals, perhaps including a new distributional goal for themselves.

As we noted earlier, setting poverty lines brings one to a confrontation with the elasticity of the poverty concept. Poverty is a condition that is difficult to define or characterize. It is relative rather than absolute; it is essentially qualitative rather than quantitative; it is to a certain extent subjective rather than objective; it refers to the general condition of man rather than a specific facet of his existence. We might agree that by some very broad definitions we are all poor (perhaps in spirit) and that even the most fortunate among us miss something of the abundant life which both secular and religious teachings hold out as ideal.

Before 1900, poverty meant pauperism or dependency, but gradually the term was broadened to encompass all insufficiency and some insecurity of income. More recently, some observers have emphasized psychological aspects (lack of self-esteem) and social attributes (lack of esteem by others) of poverty, thus harking back to the earlier emphasis on dependency. Some identify it as antisocial behavior or cultural patterns. Still others insist that poverty means lack of participation and lack of political power. The income definition of poverty does not exclude these noneconomic or cultural considerations as they relate to the low-income population. (What it does ignore is a "culture of poverty," i.e., a behavior pattern manifesting alienation from the rest of the community and a short time horizon, which may persist beyond the time income

---

[16]See comments by Margaret Reid in *Hearings on the Economic Opportunity Act of 1964,* Senate Select Committee on Poverty, 88th Congr., 2d Sess., pp. 292–93. She says this is like Humpty-Dumpty's saying that "when I use a word, it means what I mean it to mean—neither more nor less." This is reminiscent of a comment by Joseph Schumpeter. "Class,". he said, "is . . . a creation of the researcher [and] owes its existence to his organizing touch" (*Imperialism and Social Classes* [New York: World, 1955], p. 105).

is low.) It has the great advantage over other definitions that income poverty can be measured (or, more properly, *indicated*) more readily. Consider the difficulties of measuring the lack of self-esteem, lack of esteem by others, deviant behavior patterns, and lack of political power. Of course, it is true that defining poverty in income terms emphasizes policies that will change income and implies that change in income will cause a change in the psychological, social, and political variables. It assumes that the culture or subculture of poverty is more often an adaptation to limited opportunity than it is an independent and causal agent of low income.

Booth was an early social researcher who argued that "poverty is not an amorphous, intangible, pseudoreligious problem, but a concrete situation capable of economic definition and worthy of scientific scrutiny."[17] Some steps are made in Booth's direction by undertaking to objectify (that is, measure in terms of dollars) what is originally a subjective matter. Attributing extensive measures to intensive magnitudes is necessary to many operations in the social as well as the physical sciences, e.g., heat is measured by a thermometer, production is measured by an index, unemployment is measured by an activity test. Selecting an extensive measure is essentially arbitrary, but a consensus is reached so that experiment may proceed and predictive control may be advanced. In the case of poverty, there are two aspects of indirectness in measurement. One is the shift away from saying that people *feel* poor to saying that they have an income so low as to indicate that they may feel poor. The second is the assertion that even though a particular income definition may include some who are not as poor as some left out, it may nonetheless properly indicate changes in the total number who are poor.

The original consensus among experts in government on such an extensive measure was that a minimally acceptable level of consumer satisfactions could be met by the typically situated family of four persons with $3000 or more of total money income. The rationale for that mark was that at levels of income below $3000 a majority of families did not consume an adequate and nutritious diet. $3000 was noted as three times the minimum food budget for a family of four. This rationale is not superior in any logical sense to the method followed by the Bureau of Labor Statistics in pricing a basket of goods and services required to live "decently." It happens, however, that this leads to a figure considerably higher than $3000. The method selected then yields a hypothetical estimate: If all families had the same needs or desires and the same

---

[17]Cited in Robert Bremner, *From the Depths* (New York: New York University Press, 1964), p. 81.

resources other than total money income, then 9.3 million families would have been poor in 1962.

A smaller hypothetical number could be said to be poor if either a lower total money income, or $3000 of consumption expenditures, or $3000 of *personal* income (which includes such nonmoney income as home-produced food and imputed rent) were used as the standard for need. It should be noted that the shift from money income to either consumption expenditures or personal income is tantamount to a lowering of the poverty line just as surely as is adopting a lower money-income line. On the other hand, one could, as a matter of judgment, raise the number counted as poor by (for example) raising the total money-income line.

To get back to more neutral ground, one could set the line in terms of disposable personal income plus and minus interpersonal gifts and plus capital gains and free public services. Such a definition would capture changes in well-being associated with changes in free public services and changes in income and payroll taxes. The official poverty lines are stated in terms of total money income before direct taxes, but they took account of the 1962 tax system in the sense that they represent the income level at which most families did, in fact, get a nutritious diet. The lines are revised year by year as consumer prices change. Some, but not all, tax changes are caught in the price adjustment to poverty lines. A tax change which lowers or raises consumer prices is caught, but one which increases or decreases disposable but not pretax income of the poor is not. The same thing is true of a nonmoney transfer change, such as the introduction of Medicare. This shortcoming could only be remedied by going back to the original basis for setting the lines, namely finding that pretax income level at which most families of a given size do in fact purchase a nutritious diet. The point about free public services is worth further comment. It would appear to be an emerging goal with regard to such services as education, and perhaps health care, that the poor get a full per capita share. This means we cannot link a consideration of such services in with money income, concerning which our goal is much more modest. Simply achieving a national minimum income will not yield the per capita share of these services.

One could, quite sensibly, shift from annual income to an average of several years of income.[18] The possibilities for variation are infinite, and complete realism in accounting for all differences in needs and

---

[18]How much social concern should there be for the family which is only briefly in the poverty-income range? How far should government go in offsetting irregularly low incomes?

resources is beyond reach. The case method of detailed description of individual family situations is a valuable addition to, but is no substitute for, demographic analysis. Such analysis, when aimed at causal factors or at changes over time, will not necessarily be helped by a great number of separate classifications. In practice, analysis is limited by presently available data.

Accordingly, in this book we use as our reference point the total money income line, with adjustment for changes in consumer price levels, because it is the only one for which time series by relevant demographic characteristics are available. However, it is helpful to know the directions in which our understanding of poverty is biased by the particular poverty line in use, and we comment on adjustments for family size, income variability, changes in free public services and in taxation, and other factors where appropriate.

James Tobin recently commented on the political significance of a specific goal:

> The Federal "war on poverty," whatever else it has accomplished, has established an official measure of the prevalence of poverty in the United States. Adoption of a specific quantitative measure, however arbitrary and debatable, will have durable and far-reaching political consequences. Administrations will be judged by their success or failure in reducing the officially measured prevalence of poverty. So long as any families are found below the official poverty line, no politician will be able to claim victory in the war on poverty or ignore the repeated solemn acknowledgments of society's obligation to its poorer members. A similarly binding commitment to a specific measure of full employment, the adoption of 4 percent unemployment as the "interim target" of the Kennedy administration in 1961, strengthened the political forces on the side of expansionary fiscal and monetary policy in the early 1960's.[19]

Antipoverty goal setting is not complete until two other targets are stated. Neither has been stated by any administration up to the end of 1970. These are (1) a yearly rate of moving people across the line, and (2) a yearly rate of closing the poverty-income gap. Any responsible goal setting will give attention to specifics and to the possible. We do not select an infinite rate of economic growth or zero percent unemployment as our goal. In a later chapter we explore possible rates of poverty reduction and conclude that it would be reasonable to aim for the elimination of poverty by 1976.

---

[19]"Raising the Incomes of the Poor," in Kermit Gordon, ed., *Agenda for the Nation* (Washington, D.C.: Brookings Institution, 1970), p. 83.

WHO ARE THE POOR?

Setting a poverty line enables us to quantify the problem and to indicate change over time. More immediately it makes it possible to identify the several parts of the problem by answering the questions: Who are the poor, where do they live, and how are they circumstanced?

Twenty-three million, or 12 percent, of Americans were poor in 1968 (see Figure 3.1). One way to envision our poverty population is "just like the rest of us only more so." This group includes some with almost any characteristic you could name, but it includes an unusually large number of persons with certain characteristics. Thus aged persons were overrepresented in poverty and made up one-fifth of the poor. Women living alone and persons in families headed by women were

Figure 3.1.   Number of poor persons and incidence of poverty, 1948–68.

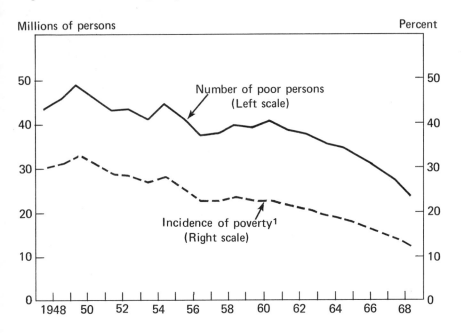

[1]Poor persons as percent of total noninstitutional population.

Note: Poverty is defined by the social security administration poverty-income standard source.

Source: Council of Economic Advisers, *Annual Report* (1969), p. 154.

similarly overrepresented and comprised over one-third of the poverty group. Those in families headed by nonaged disabled men numbered about one million. Adding up all the persons in these households headed by an aged or disabled person or by a woman yields a total of 56 percent, which indicates that over half the poor are in groups we expect to have low rates of labor-force participation. These groups, while not increasing in absolute numbers, are becoming relatively more important within the poverty population year by year.

However, we should not leap to the conclusion that work is atypical for the poor. Thirty-nine percent of persons in poor families were in families headed by a person who worked all year, 29 percent were in families where the head worked part of the year, and only 32 percent were in families (in most cases headed by women) where the head did not work at all. Seventy-seven percent of poor families have at least one earner, and 37 percent have two or more earners.

One thing that markedly distinguishes the poor from the nonpoor population is the frequency of limited educational attainment. Two-thirds of poor family heads have no more than eight grades of education. In the general population, only one-third have such limited education. The children of the poor, who numbered 12.5 million in 1966 and who thus made up almost one-sixth of the nation's children, are going to have a much higher average educational attainment than their parents, but a lower attainment than the nonpoor in their age group. Over half the poor children were in families with four or more children.

Only 13 percent of the poor are farm residents. On the other hand, 40 percent live in nonmetropolitan, nonfarm areas; 18 percent live in suburbs, and a little less than one-third of the nation's poor live in central cities of metropolitan areas. The incidence or frequency of poverty is about the same for the central cities as it is for the nation. The poor in the cities are not notably different from the poor outside the cities except that more of them are nonwhite. The region of the country which is most overrepresented among the poor is the South, which includes almost half of the nation's poor. The state with the largest number of poor is Texas and the state with the highest frequency of poverty is Mississippi.

About one-third of the poor are nonwhites, almost all of whom are Negroes. This percentage is almost unchanged from ten years ago, which indicates that the frequency of poverty for nonwhites has been falling in a way parallel to the frequency for whites. This is least true for the Indians. In 1959, 55 percent of all nonwhites were poor, but in 1967, only 35 percent were poor. This is still dramatically higher than the poverty rate for whites in 1967 of 11 percent. Alarming, too, is the fact that almost half of all nonwhite children are being reared in poverty.

A minority of the poor are on public assistance rolls. That is, in 1967 only about one-third received Old Age Assistance, Aid to the Blind or Disabled, Aid to Families with Dependent Children, or General Assistance. By 1970, however, about one-half of the poor were recipients of public assistance. This change is largely due to a rapid growth in the Aid to Families with Dependent Children program. Most of those who are not on assistance are not eligible for any assistance and will not be unless the present system of eligibility by "category" (which quite effectively excludes families headed by able-bodied men) is radically altered. Other types of transfer payments, including Social Security, Unemployment Compensation, Workmen's Compensation, and Veterans' Benefits are received by the poor as well as the nonpoor. About one-third of all households receive a public cash transfer of some kind, and it appears that the poor population would be at least 20 million larger and the poverty income gap would be at least $10 billion greater in the absence of such transfers. For those who remain poor, transfer income is almost half of total income, and wage income is about half, with entrepreneurial and property income making up the balance. Our present system of transfers is heavily weighted in favor of the aged and the broken families and does relatively little for those who are just plain poor and members of intact families.

But it is important to note that we have been talking about heavily overlapping groups and hence have both overidentified and misidentified the poor. Any simple breakdown suffers from incompleteness as in the fable of the three blind men and the elephant. For example, to say that the poor are largely old, from broken families, and nonwhite is true but dangerously incomplete and seriously misleading. One could equally well say the poor are largely children, southerners, and rural nonfarm residents—or that they are largely poorly educated.

The more one looks at the data, the more qualifications one sees to any simple cross-sectional breakdown. The impressions one gets from a look at who the poor are at a moment in time need to be modified by a look at how the poor are changing over time. For example, the rural farm poor have been declining in relative importance, nonwhites have been moving out of poverty at just about the same rate as whites; female heads and aged persons have not been getting out of poverty at a good rate.

Some misleading categorizations arise out of data shortcomings. For example, the importance of the aged among the poor is often grossly overstated by failure to adjust the data for family size and imputed rent. This means that children are undercounted. A serious data deficiency exists with regard to illness, disability, intelligence, emotional stability, and related personal characteristics as they relate to poverty. Also, relatively few of the poor family heads are *technically* defined as "unemployed" at any time; a clearer relationship would be shown by using weeks of unemployment in a year. Categorization is sometimes presented in an effort to be persuasive. Sometimes it is meant to connote causality. One might do well to classify categories as causal or noncausal. For example, should farm residence be listed as either a causal or handicapping characteristic?

In describing the poor it is often necessary to anticipate misconceptions such as that most of the poor are nonwhite or unemployed or are in the "pockets of poverty" in a few locations or are victims of automation or that all poorly educated persons are poor. Similarly, it is necessary to disengage the problem of poverty from other current problems. Poverty is not the same as the problem of discrimination or of old age or of unemployment or of farm prices. Most nonwhites are not poor. Neither are most of those unemployed or most farmers poor.

One of the most important distinctions to make is that between a depressed area and a group of poor people. There is a great tendency to think that the way to reduce poverty is to redevelop a geographic area. One could miss the mark terribly by deciding to spend money where the incidence of poverty is high. For one thing, only a small part of the country's poor are in such regions. The most common error in describing the poor is to confuse the incidence of poverty with the composition of poverty. One must present the full picture. For example, it can be said that one-half of northern Wisconsin is poor, but it should be added that only one-tenth of Wisconsin's poor are found there. One-seventh of the nation's poor are in Appalachia, but 70 percent of the residents of Appalachia are not poor.

Many of the poor possess no easily marked "handicapping" characteristic, aside from limited education. Many are in nonfarm families headed by a regularly employed white male. Almost without exception, the majority of persons in the handicapped groups (e.g., the aged and the nonwhites) are not poor. Most (65 percent) of the families headed by a person with less than eight grades of education are not poor. In only one state, namely Mississippi, does the incidence of poverty approach 50 percent. One is seriously misled if one thinks of the poor as including the dominant part of any broad demographic group. In many ways the poor population is only a slightly distorted cross-section of the general population. As we said before, the poor are like other Americans, only more so.

The diversity of people in poverty suggests that there are numerous causes of poverty and that there may well be numerous remedies.

YEAR-TO-YEAR CHANGES IN THE NUMBER OF THE POOR

Poverty is reduced when the number of people exiting from poverty exceeds the number entering. Some insight into this process is afforded by a special tabulation of the Census sample survey that shows incomes of families for two successive years. Estimates derived from that tabulation are shown in diagram form in Figure 3.2. In 1962 there were 9.3 million families in poverty; in 1963 the number was down to 9.0 million. It appears that approximately 70 percent of those families with money incomes under $3000 (no adjustment made for family size) in 1962 were also present and poor in 1963. About 6 percent (400,000) of the 1962 poor families were dissolved by death or otherwise, and about 23 percent moved to a higher income class. Most of the latter group moved to income classes only slightly above $3000, and most of them had an income average for the two years of under $3000. The other side of the process is that the 1963 poor group was largely (70 percent) made up of the families who were poor in 1962. It includes some (about 23 percent) who descended from above-poverty income levels and a small number (about 7 percent) who came out of newly formed and immigrant families. The net reduction by 300,000 in the number of poor families is explained by the facts that (1) the number of poor families dissolved exceeded the number of poor families newly created by approximately 200,000 and (2) the number of families rising out of poverty to above-poverty income levels exceeded the number descending from above-poverty income levels by about 100,000.[20]

The exits from poverty reflect temporary movements in the incomes of many from one year to another owing to unemployment, illness, or disability; part-period incomes of families formed during the year; and the risks of enterprise for many of the self-employed. They also reflect more permanent movements up the occupational and income ladders as people become more productive with added experience on the job. The extent to which the rate of exits from poverty depends upon these and

---

[20]For a definitive study of year-to-year changes in 1965–66, see Terence F. Kelly, "Factors Affecting Poverty: A Gross Flow Analysis," *Technical Studies,* President's Commission on Income Maintenance Programs (Washington, D.C.: Government Printing Office, 1970), pp. 1–81.

Figure 3.2.   Changes in poverty, 1962–63 (millions of families)

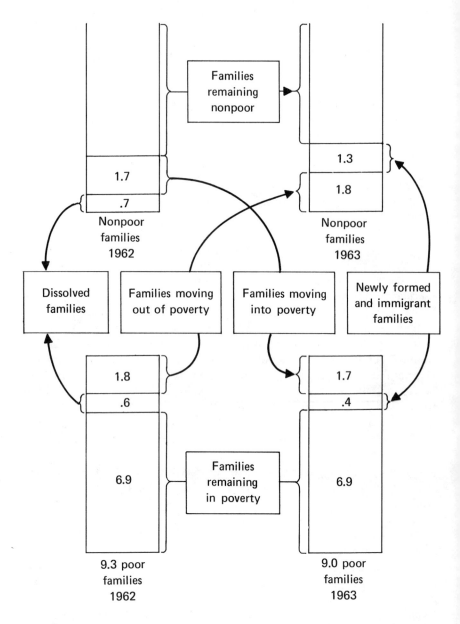

Source: *Economic Report of the President, 1965* (Washington, D.C.: Government Printing Office, 1965), derived from Table 20, p. 165.

other factors is indicated in Table 3.2, which shows variation in the persistence of poverty by selected characteristics of families. The persistence of poverty appears to be lowest among those in the prime working ages, reflecting the experience factor, and among those unemployed in the 1962 base year, reflecting the temporary nature of their lack of work. The persistence of poverty is greater than average for non-whites, families headed by women, and persons not in the labor force.

Table 3.2.   Persistence of Poverty, 1962–63

Selected characteristics	Percent in poverty in 1962 also in poverty in 1963
All families	69
Age of head	
14–24	62
25–34	55
35–44	53
45–54	63
55–64	71
65 and over	80
Color of head	
White	67
Nonwhite	76
Nonworking head	83
Female head	76

Source: *Economic Report of the President, 1965* (Washington, D.C.: Government Printing Office, 1965), Table 19, p. 164.

But just as there are many who exit from poverty, another slightly smaller group slides back into poverty every year. Presumably the newly unemployed, older family heads, and the ill and disabled are most important among those retreating into poverty. Thus it is important not only to increase the number of exits from poverty but to bolster the defenses against backsliding into poverty.

In 1947 the number of poor persons in the United States was 42 million; in 1957 there were 37 million; and in 1967 the number of poor persons was down to 25 million. Figure 3.1 shows that the rate of poverty reduction has been variable. In 1947–49, in 1953–54, and in 1956–60 the rate of reduction was zero or negative. The most rapid reduction occurred in 1949–51, 1954–56, and 1964–67, all periods of rapid growth in national employment and output. Similarly, the more substantial reduction in poverty in the second postwar decade than in the first is associated with a more favorable general economic experience.

At the same time that the number of persons in poverty has been falling, the poverty-income gap has been shrinking at a rate of about half a billion dollars a year. In 1959 this gap, which is the amount by which the actual income of the poor fell short of the income they would have if all had incomes at the Social Security Administration guideline levels, stood at $13.7 billion. In 1965 it was $11.2 billion. In 1968 the gap was $9.8 billion (see Table 3.3).

Table 3.3.   The Poverty Gap, 1959 and 1968: Total Difference between Actual and Required Income of All Households Below the Poverty Level

| Type of household | Poor households | | | | Dollar deficit | | | |
| | Number (millions) | | Percentage distribution | | Amount (billions) | | Percentage distribution | |
	1959	1968	1959	1968	1959	1968	1959	1968
Total	13.2	9.7	100.0	100.0	$13.7	$9.8	100.0	100.0
Unrelated individuals	4.9	4.7	37.2	48.2	3.8	3.4	28.2	34.5
Families	8.3	5.0	62.8	51.8	9.9	6.4	71.8	65.5

Source: U.S. Bureau of the Census, *Poverty in the United States, 1959 to 1968,* Current Population Reports, Consumer Income, Ser. P–60, No. 68 (December 31, 1969), Table F, p. 6.

In the next chapter we shift attention to changes over ten-year periods and look first at changes in the composition of the population.

PART B

Reducing Income Poverty, 1947–1967

Chapter 4

CHANGES IN THE COMPOSITION OF THE POPULATION

INTRODUCTION

In this chapter and the two following, we seek understanding of and quantitative information on how the number of persons in income poverty is reduced. We shall not be concerned with explaining how an individual family may have escaped poverty, but rather with broad changes which alter the probabilities that large numbers of people having fixed attitudes and motivations will be poor. In other words, we are dealing with certain statistical determinants of poverty. In most of the discussion which follows we assume constant economic growth and a constant percentage of unemployment.

We can, conceptually at least, separate three kinds of change. The first is change in the composition of the population. If there is a relative increase in a part of the population having a low frequency of poverty, e.g., families headed by men aged 35–45 years, then we can say there has been a population change which favors poverty reduction.

The second (discussed in chap. 5) is changes people make in search of higher incomes. If per capita production is rising, either because of increased productivity per hour of work or because of more hours being worked by more workers per thousand people, then the possibility that poverty will be reduced is improved. We can detect responses people make to possibilities for higher income by observing their shift from lower- to higher-income occupations, industries, and regions. We can also observe that there are changing frequencies of poverty within occupations, industries, and regions. These changing frequencies reflect the process of economic growth.

A thid change that may explain poverty reduction, change in income redistribution, is the subject of chapter 6. Certainly, a rise in the share of income received by the lowest fifth of families would result in a more rapid reduction of poverty, all other things remaining the same. Since transfer of income is unusually important for the low-income group, we are interested in changes that occur in the level and sharing of transfers and the taxes that are necessary to pay for them. Over and above the money payments called transfers, are transfers of goods and services like education and health services. While these are not ordinarily counted as income and do not appear as directly contributing to the reduction of poverty, they, along with money transfers, do make it possible for people to respond to opportunities to earn higher incomes and hence to escape from poverty. Thus part of this year's poverty reduction may be attributable to transfers of money or of goods and services made one or more decades earlier.

Changes in population composition, income level, and income redistribution may interact in ways that strengthen the power of each to reduce poverty, or they may work against each other. Our study, then, is directed toward broad changes which bear on the possibility of continuing reduction in poverty. Do these changes indicate that there has been a fundamental shift in the nature of the low-income problem? Is it reasonable to expect that the future rate of change in numbers in poverty will be about the same as it has been in the past? A leading question which motivates all the others asked above is, what preventive and remedial programs can we improve or initiate to hasten the complete victory over poverty?

CHANGE IN FAMILY SIZE

Between 1947 and 1957 the size of consumer units (families) changed in such a way as to encourage an increase in the number of poor consumer units and poor persons.[1] The greatest increase in numbers of consumer units over the ten-year period occurred near the extremes of the family sizes where the frequency of poverty was unusually high—families of one, two, five, and six persons (compare columns 1 and 2 in Table 4.1). The increase in these particular family sizes would have had the effect of increasing the total number of low-income persons if no other changes had taken place. However, the frequency of low income fell dramatically —by one-third or more—for three-, four-, and five-person families and less dramatically for other family sizes, causing the number of low-income *persons* to fall from 26 to 19 percent of all persons (compare

---

[1]Tables 4.1 through 5.2 are based on poverty lines turing around $2000 (1947 prices) for a family of four. The results, therefore, are somewhat different from calculations based on the official poverty line of $3000 (1962 prices) for a family of four persons.

Table 4.1. Distribution and Frequency of Low-Income Consumer Units, by Size of Unit (Selected Years)

Size of consumer units (no. of persons)	Number in group (millions)				Number of low-income units[a] (millions)				Incidence of low income (percent)			
	1947 (1)	1957 (2)	1962 (3)	1967 (4)	1947 (5)	1957 (6)	1962 (7)	1967 (8)	1947 (9)	1957 (10)	1962 (11)	1967 (12)
1	8.1	10.3	11.0	13.1	4.1	4.4	4.2	4.0	51	43	40	30
2	11.7	14.3	15.0	16.9	2.7	2.5	2.4	1.9	23	17	16	11
3	9.6	9.5	9.8	10.3	1.8	1.2	1.1	0.8	19	13	11	8
4	7.4	8.8	9.4	9.5	1.5	1.0	1.1	0.6	20	11	11	6
5	4.2	5.5	6.1	6.2	0.9	0.8	0.8	0.4	21	15	12	6
6	2.2	2.9	3.4	3.5	0.7	0.7	0.6	0.4	32	24	17	11
7 or more	2.3	2.6	3.3	3.4	1.0	1.0	1.0	0.7	44	38	31	21
Total consumer units	45.3	54.0	58.0	62.9	12.7	11.6	11.2	8.8	28.0	21.5	19.2	14.0
Total persons	144.6	168.3	185.3	195.0	37.6	32.2	32.6	22.6	26	19	18	12

[a] Low-income units are defined as those below variable minimum incomes for the several family sizes with $2000 (1947 prices) for a family of 4 as a base.

Source: Data for 1947 and 1957 are obtained from R. J. Lampman, Joint Economic Committee Study Paper No. 12, *The Low Income Population and Economic Growth*. Data for 1961, 1962, and 1963 are derived from U.S. Bureau of the Census, *Current Population Survey*, Ser. P-60.

columns 9 and 10).[2] While the number of large families increased in the total population, the number of such families in the poor population fell, partly due to an increase in the number of workers per family.

Between 1957 and 1962 the change in family size also worked to bring about an increase in the number of poor persons, and this time the demographic change was less dominated by incidence changes. While small families increased by less than 10 percent, families of six and seven or more increased by about 20 percent. The startling result is that the number of poor persons was 32.2 million in 1957 and 32.6 million in 1962. In other words, the absolute number of persons in poverty, when the poverty definition takes account of variation in family size, was virtually unchanged from 1957 through 1962.

During 1962–67 family size changes were less unfavorable for poverty reduction. Although one- and two-person families increased disproportionately, the number of largest-sized families increased only slightly. These demographic changes combined with sharp drops in incidence rates, especially for four- and five-person families, to lower the number in poverty (as defined here) to 22.6 million persons.

CHANGE IN AGE OF FAMILY HEADS

Aged heads of consumer units increased in numbers at twice the rate of heads of all ages from 1947 to 1957 (see Table 4.2). This would have had the effect of increasing the number of low-income units very substantially if no changes in the frequency of low income had occurred within any age group. In fact, however, within some age groups there were large

---

[2]Some readers may be interested in a more specific answer as to the effects of the changes shown in Table 4.1. Population change alone would have raised the number of low-income units from 12.7 million in 1947 (see col. 5) to 15.1 million in 1957, and changes among the family size groups would have added another 0.3 million units. The changes in incidence offset both the population growth and the shift among the family size groups and dropped the number of low-income units from a potential of 15.4 million to the actual number of 11.6 million in 1957. The average size of low-income units fell from 2.87 to 2.79 persons. Making the calculations in terms of the persons in these units gives the following findings: Population change alone would have increased the number of low-income persons from 37.6 million in 1947 to 43.6 million in 1957. The movement into different family size groups would have added another 2.6 million to raise the total to 46.2 million, but the low incidence rates noted above dropped the actual number of low-income persons to 32.2 million in 1957.

Table 4.2.   Percentage Change in Number of Families, by Age of Heads,
1947–67

	1947–57	1957–67	1957–62	1962–67
All families	16	14	8	5
Under 24	22	41	14	24
25–34	12	7	0	8
35–44	16	7	9	−3
45–54	19	12	4	7
55–64	8	23	10	10
65 and over	31	22	17	4

Source: Table 4.3.

changes in incidence, particularly in the group aged 25–34, where the incidence rate fell from 24 to 12 percent. Population growth alone would have raised the number of low-income families from 10.4 million to 11.8 million (Table 4.3). Changes in ages of family heads would have raised the number to 12.1 million. Incidence changes dropped it to the actual number of 8.7 million low-income families in 1957. It is notable that there was virtually no decline in the incidence rate for families headed by aged persons. Similarly, incidence rates did not fall much for any age groups of unattached individuals, with the consequence that the number of unattached individuals with under $1000 (1947 prices) of income actually rose between 1947 and 1957.

Change in age composition also worked against poverty reduction between 1957 and 1967, with above-average increases in the number of aged and young family heads. The pattern of change was markedly different between the first and second halves of the ten-year period, with a shift from old to young as the rapid-growth age groups. This presages a period ahead in which population change may be favorable to poverty reduction.

Thus it would seem that an important factor in reducing the total number of low-income units and persons was the reduction of the incidence of low income among large families, which contain a large part of the population, and a relative decline in the numbers of large families. This development in turn is presumably due to (1) some realignment of fertility by income class, (2) some separation of aged persons from multi-person families, and (3) some increase in the number of earners per multi-person family.

In elaboration of these three points the following considerations may be mentioned. In 1965 the fertility rate of poor wives (those with family incomes under $3000) was one-fourth higher than that of the

Table 4.3. Distribution and Frequencies of Low-Income Families and Unattached Individuals by Age of Head (Selected Years)

Families

Age of head	Number in age group (millions)				Number of low-income units (millions)				Incidence of low income (percent)			
	1947 (1)	1957 (2)	1962 (3)	1967 (4)	1947 under $2000 (5)	1957 under $2500 (6)	1962 under $2688 (7)	1967 under $2975 (8)	1947 (5)÷(1) (9)	1957 (6)÷(2) (10)	1962 (7)÷(3) (11)	1967 (8)÷(3) (12)
All families	37.3	43.6	47.0	49.8	10.4	8.7	8.1	6.2	28	20	17	12
Under 24	1.8	2.2	2.5	3.1	0.7	0.5	0.7	0.6	39	24	27	18
25–34	8.1	9.1	9.1	9.8	2.0	1.0	1.1	0.7	25	12	12	8
35–44	8.9	10.4	11.4	11.1	2.0	1.2	1.1	0.6	22	12	10	6
45–54	8.0	9.5	9.9	10.6	1.7	1.6	1.2	0.7	21	17	12	7
55–64	6.1	6.6	7.3	8.1	1.7	1.5	1.2	1.0	28	23	17	12
65 and over	4.4	5.8	6.8	7.1	2.3	2.9	2.8	2.6	53	50	41	37

Unrelated individuals

Age of head	1947 (1)	1957 (2)	1962 (3)	1967 (4)	1947 under $920 (5)	1957 under $1157 (6)	1962 under $1244 (7)	1967 under $1377 (8)	1947 (5)÷(1) (9)	1957 (6)÷(2) (10)	1962 (7)÷(3) (11)	1967 (8)÷(3) (12)
All unattached individuals	8.0	10.2	11.0	13.1	3.7	4.1	3.8	4.0	46	40	35	31
Under 24	0.8	0.8	1.1	1.5	0.4	0.4	0.5	0.5	50	50	45	33
25–34	1.0	1.1	1.0	1.2	0.3	0.2	0.2	0.1	30	18	20	8
35–44	1.1	1.1	0.9	1.1	0.3	0.3	0.2	0.2	27	27	22	18
45–54	1.4	1.6	1.5	1.6	0.5	0.4	0.4	0.3	36	25	27	19
55–64	1.4	2.2	2.3	2.6	0.6	0.8	0.7	0.7	43	36	30	27
65 and over	2.3	3.4	4.2	5.1	1.5	1.9	1.9	2.2	65	56	45	43

Sources: For 1947–62: U.S. Bureau of the Census, Technical Paper No. 17, *Trends in the Income of Families and*

nonpoor.[3] However, it would seem that the old commonplace about the rich being outreproduced by the poor is slowly being negated. One scholar summarizes the studies of differential fertility as follows:

> The general consensus of demographers and other observers of population phenomena has been that differential fertility among various groupings within the American population has been in a process of contraction during recent decades. . . . Should this trend continue in the future, students of differential fertility some day may well be seeking explanations of a direct rather than an inverse relationship between education, occupation, and fertility.[4]

There are no available data on death rates by income class, but both infant mortality and general mortality rates are higher in lower-income occupations, regions, and educational classes. However, these differentials in death rates by class have been narrowing in recent years.[5]

Point (2), about separation of aged persons from multiperson families, has to do with the "undoubling" of families. This again is part of a long trend, in this case associated with the shift from a rural to an urban and industrialized way of life. But higher average incomes, and higher Social Security benefits in particular, may have accommodated the observably higher rate of undoubling in the postwar years. Since undoubling has the paradoxical effect of showing more low-income units as average income rises, it is important to measure changes in the low-income population in terms of persons rather than consumer units. This does not totally solve the problem, since some are "hidden" as poor in households of their nonpoor relatives until their Social Security benefits rise enough to maintain a separate (poor) household.

CHANGES IN EMPLOYMENT

Employed family heads declined as a proportion of all family heads from 1948 to 1957. This proportion declined further from 1957 to 1962, but returned to the 1957 level by 1967 (see Table 4.4). This decline, which

---

[3]U.S. Bureau of the Census, *Current Population Reports,* Ser. P-20, No. 186 (Washington, D.C.: U.S. Government Printing Office, 1969), Table 7, p. 118.

[4]Charles W. Westoff, "Differential Fertility in the United States, 1900 to 1952," *American Sociological Review* 19 (October 1954), 561.

[5]See Table 4.5 for data on changes in size of family and number of children by family income level.

Table 4.4. Distribution and Frequency of Low-Income Families, by Employment Status of Head

	Millions of families								Percent			
	1948 (1)	1957 (2)	1962 (3)	1967 (4)	1948 under $2180 (5)	1957 under $2500 (6)	1962 under $2688 (7)	1967 under $2975 (8)	1948 (5) ÷ (1) (9)	1957 (6) ÷ (2) (10)	1962 (7) ÷ (3) (11)	1967 (8) ÷ (4) (12)
Total	38.5	43.7	47.0	49.8	9.7	8.7	8.1	6.2	25	20	17	12
Employed civilians	31.9	34.5	36.9	39.5	6.4	4.5	3.9	2.4	20	13	11	6
In Armed Forces or not employed	6.6	9.2	10.1	10.3	3.3	4.2	4.2	3.8	50	45	42	37

Source: See Table 4.3.

would tend to increase the number of low-income families, is of course related to the changes described above in age and family size. Between 1948 and 1957 the number of families headed by an employed civilian rose by 8 percent, while the number of families headed by a person in the Armed Forces or not employed rose by 40 percent. Population growth alone would have increased the number of low-income families. The movement out of employment (unless offset by falling incidence rates) would have further raised the total of low-income families. However, incidence rates fell, particularly for those families headed by an employed civilian, so that the number of low-income families actually fell.[6]

More and more, the low-income groups are identified with lack of employment. While two-thirds of low-income family heads were employed civilians in 1947, only a little over one-third were in 1967. This change is in part explained by the long period of prosperity and inflation. The incomes of families headed by workers tend to rise with rising prices and wages, whereas the incomes of families living on pensions and other types of fixed incomes do not rise as rapidly as others. Similarly, the increase in number of workers per family is most likely to have occurred in those age groups where the head is typically in the labor force.

A hunch that a large part of this increase in the number of non-working low-income family heads is due to the increase in aged low-income heads is strengthened by a look back at Table 4.3. There was a 32 percent increase in the number of aged family heads and virtually no change in the incidence of low income among the aged between 1947 and 1957. The increase in aged and low-income heads was 600,000, whereas the increase in the "Armed Forces or not employed" low-income category was 900,000 over the same period (Table 4.4). The only age-sex groups showing important declines in employment between 1950 and 1957 were men under 25 and over 65.[7] Among men 65 and over, the proportion working from fifty to fifty-two weeks at full-time jobs fell from 52 to 45 percent. This decline in employment may explain the fact that the incidence of low income stayed at about 50 percent for aged families over the period in which a remarkable change was going forward in the aggregate level of old-age benefits under social insurance. The number of persons 65 and over who were receiving benefits from social

---

[6]The population increase would have raised the number of low-income units from 9.7 million to 10.9 million. The shift out of employment would have raised the number to 11.5 million. The changes in incidence rates dropped it to the actual number of 8.7 million families.

[7]U.S. Bureau of the Census, *Current Population Reports,* Ser. P–50, No. 86 (Washington, D.C.: Government Printing Office, 1958), p. 4.

insurance and related programs rose from 2.3 million in 1948 to 10.4 million in 1958.[8] Benefit rates had been substantially raised so that benefit payments under social insurance, assistance, and related programs probably accounted for more than one-third of the aggregate money income of all persons 65 years of age and older in 1958.

Alternative and overlapping explanations of the lowered employment experience, which is part of a long-term trend that reaches back at least to 1900, are:

1) It is associated with the decline of farming
2) Men over 65 are older now on the average
3) Some increase in retirement was due to increased assets and planned dissaving of those assets
4) Increases in transfer payments and higher wage rates for part-time work accommodate a desire for less employment

Table 4.5 offers another view of changes in family composition and labor-force participation. It should be noted that unattached individuals are not included in the table. Between 1947 and 1964 the average number of earners per family increased from 1.38 to 1.52. The greater part of this increase is accounted for by the fact that wives worked in only 18.6 percent of all families in 1949 but in 28.7 percent of all families in 1964. The number of workers per family has increased in all income ranges except the lowest (see Table 4.5). This means that many families moved out of the lowest fifth during 1948–64 by sending an additional family member into the labor force. At the same time, many small families or those with a disabled member were unable to increase their income, and this contributes to the disproportionate representation of unrelated individuals and disabled persons in the contemporary low-income population.

It is true that poverty is increasingly associated with nonemployment.[9] However, it is important to correct an erroneous impression concerning the importance in a given year of the working poor which is conveyed by Tables 4.4 and 4.5. These tables are based on a definition of low-income status which makes no adjustment for family size. When that adjustment is made, we find that only 40 percent of poor family

---

[8]Lenore A. Epstein, "Money Income of Aged Persons: A Ten-Year Review, 1948 and 1958," *Social Security Bulletin* (June 1959), p. 4. The average monthly OASI benefit paid to retired workers in June 1956 was $61.03.

[9]Nonemployed persons are considered not to be in the labor force; the unemployed are presumably seeking jobs.

Table 4.5. Family Composition: Fifths of Families Ranked by Size of Money Income (Selected Years)

Fifths of families	Average size of family			Average no. of children under 18 years living in family			Median age of family head			Percent of family heads age 65 and over		
	1947	1957	1964	1948[a]	1957	1964	1947	1957	1964	1947	1957	1964
Lowest	3.18	3.22	3.13	1.14	1.22	1.19	49.8	52.2	51.7	26.2	32.3	34.0
2	3.45	3.55	3.56	1.29	1.47	1.46	43.2	46.7	45.2	10.3	13.8	15.5
3	3.57	3.72	3.79	1.31	1.57	1.64	42.5	42.5	43.3	6.4	7.0	7.3
4	3.63	3.74	3.84	1.20	1.49	1.57	43.7	43.2	44.8	5.9	5.5	6.3
Highest	4.01	3.78	3.82	1.04	1.30	1.33	48.1	45.9	47.4	8.8	6.1	7.1
Total	3.57	3.60	3.63	1.20	1.41	1.44	45.5	46.1	46.5	11.5	12.9	14.0

Fifths of families	Percent of families with female heads			Average no. of earners in family			Percent of husband-wife families in paid labor force			Percent of heads not in labor force, unemployed, or in Armed Forces		
	1947	1957	1964	1947	1957	1964	1949[a]	1957	1964	1948[a]	1957	1964
Lowest	18.2	21.9	24.4	0.97	1.05	0.96	10.3	11.9	11.8	24.3	48.2	51.5
2	10.9	10.5	12.5	1.21	1.38	1.40	15.2	19.5	23.3	11.3	24.7	24.3
3	7.4	6.2	6.3	1.31	1.47	1.56	15.7	22.3	28.6	6.7	14.2	12.1
4	6.6	4.6	4.4	1.55	1.69	1.77	24.8	32.2	38.1	5.3	11.1	9.1
Highest	6.8	3.6	3.7	1.85	1.89	1.94	27.2	38.2	41.6	5.3	9.2	7.2
Total	10.0	9.4	10.2	1.38	1.50	1.52	18.6	24.8	28.7	10.6	21.5	20.8

[a]Information for 1947 was not available.
Source: U.S. Bureau of the Census, Technical Paper No. 17, *Trends in the Income of Families and Persons in the United States: 1947–1964* (Washington, D.C.: U.S. Government Printing Office, 1967), pp. 20–29.

heads (2.4 out of 6.1 million) did not work in 1966.[10] If we think of
persons rather than families in poverty, we find a still lower association
with nonemployment; only 32 percent of all poor persons were in households where the head did not work during the year (7.8 out of 24.8
million). Most of the poor (16.6 out of the 24.8 million poor persons in
families) were in families whose head worked part or all of the year.
(No information is available for unrelated individuals.) Of these persons,
12.7 million were outside the categories of aged and broken families.
At the same time, over half the persons in broken families were in
families where the head worked. This line of inquiry is related to how
many poor persons receive public assistance. Most of the poor (21.5
out of 29.7 million persons) did not receive public assistance in 1966.
Of this 21.5 million, 5.4 million were in aged and broken families, but
16.1 million were not in these categories. Most of the latter group were
probably not eligible for any assistance.

CHANGES IN RACIAL COMPOSITION

Between 1947 and 1967 the number of nonwhite families increased
almost twice as fast as white families, that is, 60 compared to 31 percent.
For unrelated individuals the difference was less marked (80 versus
61 percent). Since the frequency of poverty is much higher for nonwhites,
this greater rate of population growth among nonwhites worked against
poverty reduction. The overall population growth over the years 1947
to 1967 leads to a prediction of 14.0 million families in poverty in 1967;
the differentially high increase in numbers of nonwhites would lead
one to expect a total of 14.5 million. In fact, however, the great declines
in incidence of poverty experienced by both whites and nonwhites
resulted in only 6.2 million families being in poverty in 1967.[11]

CHANGES IN COMPOSITION BY SEX
OF FAMILY HEAD

Families headed by women have not increased as a share of all families
over the twenty-year period under review (see Table 4.5), hence this

---

[10]Mollie Orshansky, "Counting the Poor: Before and After Federal Income-
Support Programs," in U.S. Joint Committee, *Old Age Income Assurance: A
Compendium* (Washington, D.C.: Government Printing Office, 1967), Part II,
p. 214, Table 9.
[11]*Consumer Income,* "Income in 1967 of Families in the U.S."

cannot be considered to be a factor working against poverty reduction. However, it is notable that the incidence of poverty improved relatively little for this group of families. Table 4.5 shows that families headed by women were only 18.2 percent of the lowest fifth of families in 1947, but were 24.4 percent of the lowest fifth in 1964. Other data, not shown here, reveal that the incidence of poverty among families headed by women was 47 percent in 1947, 49 percent in 1957, and 37 percent in 1967.

SUMMARY

Between 1947 and 1967 all the changes in the composition of the population reviewed above worked against poverty reduction. Poverty was reduced *in spite of* (1) relatively rapid increases in those family sizes where poverty is most common, (2) an unfavorable change in the ages of family heads, (3) a relative decrease in the number of families headed by persons in the labor force, and (4) a disproportionate increase in the nonwhite population, which has a much higher incidence of poverty than does the white population.

Each change may be said to have contributed about 500,000 families to the potential candidates for poverty status in 1967. However, categories overlap (e.g., age changes are related to labor-force changes), so that the combined effect must have been considerably less than 4 times 500,000 or 2 million families.

Chapter 5

MOVES PEOPLE MAKE IN SEARCH OF HIGHER INCOMES

Four principal factors made possible the drop in the percentage of low-income family units: shifts from rural to nonrural residence, shifts into higher-paying occupations, shifts into higher-paying industries, and shifts to higher-income states and regions. These four factors are obviously interrelated and reflect the process of economic growth.

MOVEMENT OFF FARMS

The leading change from 1947 to 1957 was the absolute reduction in the number of rural-farm families from 6.5 million to 4.8 million (see Table 5.1). Population change alone would have raised the total number of low-income families from 10.1 million in 1947 to 11.8 million in 1957; the movement off farms alone would have reduced this to 10.2 million; and low-income incidence change (which happened only in the case of urban families) caused it to drop to its actual 1957 count of 8.7 million families. It is worth special mention that the frequency of low income among both farm families and farm individuals did not fall at all over the decade. Progress on this count was achieved only by the movement off farms and by simultaneously raising incomes in nonfarm residence groups. The failure of farm incomes to improve is related in part to age. Younger persons leave and older persons stay on farms. The result is that the median age of farm family heads is considerably higher than that of nonfarm heads.

The movement off farms continued through 1957–67. A new Census definition of farm residence requires that we use a new series, starting in 1959, which shows the number of farm families falling from 3.8 million in 1959 to 2.7 million in 1967. Over that period, population growth alone would have raised the number of low-income families from 8.4 million to 9.5 million, and the shift off farms would have reduced that number to 8.8 million. Beyond that, however, striking drops in incidence

Table 5.1. Distribution and Frequency of Low-Income Families, by Place of Residence (Selected Years)

Residence	Number in group (millions)		Number of low-income units (millions)		Incidence rates (percent)	
	1947 (1)	1957 (2)	Under $2000 (1947) (3)	Under $2500 (1957) (4)	1947 (3 ÷ 1) (5)	1957 (4 ÷ 2) (6)
Total	37.3	43.7	10.1	8.7	27	20
Urban	22.5	27.5	4.5	4.1	20	15
Rural nonfarm	8.3	11.4	1.7	2.3	20	20
Rural farm	6.5	4.8	3.3	2.4	51	50
	1959	1967	Under $2600 (1959)	Under $2975 (1967)	1959	1967
Total	45.1	49.8	8.4	6.2	19	12
Rural nonfarm	41.3	47.1	6.7	5.5	16	12
	3.8	2.7	1.7	0.7	45	26

Source: See Table 4.3.

of poverty, on farms as well as off, brought the actual number of low-income families down to 6.2 million.

MOVEMENT INTO HIGHER-PAYING OCCUPATIONS AND INDUSTRIES

Both occupational and industrial population shifts contributed to the drop in the number of low-income families in 1948–57. In both cases population growth alone would have raised the number from 6.4 to 6.9 million families (ignoring those out of the labor force), but movement (without incidence changes) would have lowered the number to 5.8 million (occupational shifts) or 5.9 million (industry shifts). In fact, a whole series of drops in incidence in many occupations and industries (though not notably in agriculture or finance) cut the number of low-income families to 4.5 million (see Tables 5.2 and 5.3).

Similar shifts occurred between 1957 and 1967. Population change alone would have raised the number of low-income families to 7.9 million in 1967. The shift from low-paying to higher-paying occupations would by itself have lowered the number to 6.0 million. In fact, however, the incidence of low income fell in every industry and occupation and brought the number of low-income families to 3.0 million.

It is interesting to compare the information in Table 5.3 with the following. In 1965, 5.5 million men and women reported that they worked fifty to fifty-two weeks, usually full time, for money earnings of less than $2500. These 5.5 million were 12 percent of all the persons who were fully employed in that year. For men, the frequency of these low earnings was 43 percent in agriculture and under 10 percent in all other industries. For women, the frequency was 25 percent or higher only in trade and service and finance.[1]

MOVEMENT TO HIGHER-INCOME STATES AND REGIONS

Regional shifts of population were favorable to poverty reduction betwen 1953 and 1967. Table 5.4 shows that national population growth would predict an increase in the number of low-income families from

---

[1]Vera C. Perulla, "Low Earners and Their Incomes," *Monthly Labor Review* (May 1967), pp. 35–37.

Table 5.2. Distribution and Frequency of Low-Income Families, by Occupation of Head (Selected Years)

Occupational group	Number in occupation (millions)			Number of low-income families (millions)			Incidence rates (percent)		
	1948 (1)	1957 (2)	1967 (3)	1948 (Under $2000) (4)	1957 (Under $2500) (5)	1967 (Under $2975) (6)	1948 (4 ÷ 1) (7)	1957 (5 ÷ 2) (8)	1967 (6 ÷ 3) (9)
Total employed civilians	31.9	34.5	39.5	6.4	4.5	2.4	20	13	6
Professional, technical and kindred	2.2	3.7	5.6	0.1	0.1	0.1	6	4	2
Farmers and farm managers	4.0	2.5	1.6	2.0	1.3	0.5	51	54	32
Property manager and official excluding farm	4.7	5.2	6.1	0.5	0.5	0.2	11	9	3
Clerical and kindred	2.2	2.5	3.1	0.1	0.1	0.1	7	5	4
Salesmen and saleswomen	1.6	2.0	2.2	0.2	0.1	0.1	11	7	4
Craftsmen and kindred	6.1	7.0	8.0	0.7	0.4	0.2	11	6	3
Operatives and kindred	6.3	6.6	7.7	0.8	0.6	0.2	13	9	3
Domestic service	0.3	0.3	0.3	0.2	0.2	0.1	77	69	40
Service workers excluding domestic	1.9	2.1	2.6	0.5	0.4	0.3	25	18	13
Farm laborers and foremen	0.6	0.5	0.5	0.4	0.3	0.2	68	60	34
Laborers excluding farm and name	2.0	2.0	1.8	0.6	0.4	0.2	32	22	12

Source: See Table 4.3.

Table 5.3. Distribution and Frequency of Low-Income Families, by Industry of Head (Selected Years)

Industry	Number in industry (millions)			Number of low-income families (millions)			Incidence rates (percent)		
	1948 (1)	1957 (2)	1967 (3)	1948 (Under $2000) (4)	1957 (Under $2500) (5)	1967 (Under $2975) (6)	1948 (4 ÷ 1) (7)	1957 (5 ÷ 2) (8)	1967 (6 ÷ 3) (9)
Total employed civilians	31.9	34.5	42.2[a]	6.4	4.5	3.0[a]	20	13	7[a]
Agriculture and farm	4.8	3.2	2.8	2.5	1.5	0.9	53	52	31
Mining	0.7	0.5	0.5	0.1	0.0	0.0	9	5	4
Construction	2.4	2.9	3.9	0.5	0.4	0.3	21	12	7
Manufacturing	8.8	10.3	13.2	0.8	0.5	0.4	9	5	3
Transportation	3.1	3.1	3.6	0.3	0.2	0.1	9	7	3
Wholesale	1.4	1.7	1.8	0.2	0.1	0.1	12	8	4
Retail	4.3	4.5	4.9	0.7	0.6	0.4	17	13	9
Finance	0.9	1.2	1.7	0.1	0.1	0.1	8	8	3
Business and repair service	0.8	1.2	1.3	0.2	0.2	0.1	19	14	7
Personal and domestic	1.1	1.3	1.4	0.5	0.4	0.3	42	34	24
Amusement, recreation, and related services	0.2	0.2	0.3	0.0	b	0.0	9	b	10
Professional	1.9	2.5	4.2	0.3	0.3	0.3	15	11	6
Government	1.5	1.9	2.6	0.1	0.1	0.0	6	4	2

[a]For 1967, includes Armed Forces.
[b]Not available.
Source: See Table 4.3.

Table 5.4. Distribution and Frequency of Low-Income Families, by Region (1953 and 1967), with Hypothetical Numbers for 1967

| Region | Number in region (millions) | | Percentage change | Number of families with incomes under $3000[a] (millions) | | Incidence rate (percent) | | Hypothetical number of low-income families (millions) in 1967 | |
	1953 (1)	1967 (2)	1953–67 (3)	1953 (4)	1967 (5)	1953 (6)	1967 (7)	Holding incidence rate constant (8)	Holding regional composition and incidence constant (9)
All regions	41.2	49.8	21	9.4	6.2	24	13	11.5	12.0
Northeast	10.7	12.3	15	1.5	1.1	14	9	1.7	—
North Central	12.3	14.1	14	2.3	1.5	19	11	2.7	—
South	12.3	15.0	22	4.5	2.7	37	18	5.5	—
West	5.8	8.5	46	1.1	0.8	19	9	1.6	—

[a]1967 dollars.
Sources: U.S. Bureau of the Census, *Income in 1967 of Families in the U.S.*, Table 4, p. 23, Table 20, p. 51; *Trends in Income*, Table A, p. 3.

Table 5.5. Changes in Poverty 1949–59, by State, with States Listed by Incidence of Poverty in 1949

	Rank orders poverty incidence		Change in number of families (percent)	Net migration (percent)	Change in number of poor families (percent)	Percent of nation's poor[a]		Rank in number of poor families	
	1949 (1)	1959 (2)	(3)	(4)	(5)	1949 (6)	1959 (7)	1949 (8)	1959 (9)
All States	—	—	17	—	−30	100	100	—	—
Mississippi	1	1	− 2	−20	−32	3	3	14	12
Arkansas	2	2	− 5	−23	−34	2	2	18	18
Alabama	3	4	8	−12	−31	3	3	11	11
Georgia	4	9	15	− 6	−31	4	4	8	10
South Carolina	5	3	13	−10	−24	2	2	22	19
Tennessee	6	5	11	− 8	−27	3	4	9	9
Kentucky	7	6	5	−13	−30	3	3	12	14
North Carolina	8	7	16	−10	−22	4	4	7	5
Louisiana	9	8	19	− 2	−22	3	3	15	15
Oklahoma	10	12	4	−10	−55	2	2	21	21
Florida	11	15	79	+57	+ 5	3	4	17	8
Vermont	12	21	5	−10	−46	—	—	46	46
West Virginia	13	11	− 4	−23	−29	2	2	27	27
Virginia	14	16	22	− 6	−24	3	3	16	16
Missouri	15	17	7	− 3	−34	3	3	10	12
Maine	16	22	8	− 1	−45	1	1	35	37
Texas	17	13	21	+ 1	−20	6	7	2	1
South Dakota	18	10	4	−13	−16	1	1	38	36
New Mexico	19	20	39	+ 7	−22	1	1	37	38
Arizona	20	25	71	+41	−10	1	1	36	34
Kansas	21	23	12	0	−38	1	1	28	23
Nebraska	22	18	6	− 9	−30	1	1	31	31
North Dakota	23	14	8	−18	−24	—	—	40	39
New Hampshire	24	41	14	0	−52	—	—	43	45

	poverty incidence		number of families (percent)	Net migration (percent)	number of poor families (percent)	nation's poor[a]		number of poor families	
	1949 (1)	1959 (2)	(3)	(4)	(5)	1949 (6)	1959 (7)	1949 (8)	1959 (9)
Colorado	26	28	30	+12	−32	1	1	33	32
Idaho	27	26	12	−1	−34	—	—	41	41
Minnesota	28	24	12	−3	−28	2	2	25	24
Indiana	29	29	15	+2	−35	2	2	19	20
Delaware	30	36	40	+20	−31	—	—	47	47
Rhode Island	31	34	11	−4	−41	—	—	39	40
Montana	32	27	14	−1	−27	—	—	45	42
Wisconsin	33	30	14	−2	−36	2	2	24	25
Pennsylvania	34	33	10	−5	−39	6	5	3	4
Maryland	35	40	31	+14	−34	1	1	29	29
Oregon	36	32	12	+1	−36	—	—	32	33
Utah	37	43	23	+1	−38	—	—	42	43
Ohio	38	38	19	+5	−32	4	4	5	7
Wyoming	39	35	16	−1	−30	—	—	48	48
Washington	40	39	16	+4	−34	1	1	30	30
California	41	44	41	+30	−25	5	6	4	3
Massachusetts	42	47	10	0	−48	2	2	20	26
Nevada	43	46	77	+45	−14	—	—	49	49
New York	44	45	12	+1	−39	7	6	1	2
Michigan	45	37	20	+3	−24	3	3	13	13
Illinois	46	42	13	+1	−31	4	4	6	6
Dist. of Columbia	47	31	12	−20	−36	—	—	44	44
Connecticut	48	49	28	+12	−45	1	1	34	35
New Jersey	49	48	25	+1	−36	2	2	23	23

[a]Blanks in Columns 6 and 7 indicate less than 0.5 percent.

Sources: Except for data on net migration, all data are derived from the 1950 and 1960 Censuses of Population. Net migration as a percentage of 1950 population derived from U.S. Bureau of the Census, *Current Population Reports*, Series P–25, No. 227.

9.4 million to 12.0 million. However, the regional shift without incidence changes would have caused a drop to 11.5 million. This result would have been due to the extraordinarily rapid growth of population in the West, where incidence rates were low, which more than offset the slightly above average growth in the South. In fact, however, the percentage of families with low income fell in every region, most sharply in the South and West, and the number of low-income families was reduced to 6.2 million. The share of all low-income families to be found in the South declined from 48 percent in 1953 to 44 percent in 1967.

The future geographic distribution of poverty is of course related to the present distribution of poor children; in 1960, 56 percent were found in the South, 20 percent in the North Central region, 13 percent in the Northeast, and only 11 percent in the West. The average number of children per family for these regions, respectively, was 2.8, 2.4, 2.2, and 2.4.

The incidence of poverty fell more sharply in the rich states than in the poor states, generally speaking, with the result that the range of difference was wider in 1959 than in 1949. In the poorest state, Mississippi, 70 percent of the families lived in poverty in 1949, when in the richest state, Connecticut, 20 percent lived in poverty. In 1959 the incidence rates were 52 for Mississippi and 9 for Connecticut.

A further inquiry into the effect of population movement is shown in Table 5.5, which records changes on a state-by-state basis between two recent Census years. For example, it shows that Mississippi, the state having the highest incidence of poverty in both years, had an absolute decline in population, that it experienced a net out-migration equal to 20 percent of its 1950 population, that it reduced its numbers in poverty at the same rate as the nation, and that it contained about 3 percent of the nation's poor in both years but rose in rank from fourteenth to twelfth among the states in absolute number of poor families.

By contrasting the thirteen poorest and the thirteen richest states, we find that population increases were greatest in the richest states. The poorest states had an average population gain of 13 percent while the richest states gained 23 percent. Some of the change is because the poorest group had an average rate of out-migration of 7 percent, whereas the richest group had an in-migration of 6 percent. In spite of this, the poorest group had a slightly larger share of the nation's poor in 1959 than in 1949 (36 and 34 percent). Part of the answer to the puzzle is that the rate of poverty reduction was greater in the richer states. The table suggests but does not provide clear proof that interstate mobility contributed to the nationwide reduction of poverty. We do not know, for example, whether it was poor or nonpoor people who moved out of Mississippi and out of New England. Nor can we tell for sure whether Texas would have risen to the rank of having the most poor people if it had not had an influx of population.

SUMMARY

The shifts of population between farm and nonfarm residence, and among occupations, industries, and regions all contributed to the reduction of poverty during the period under study. In other words, the direction of population movement was toward higher income. The quantitative significance of each of these shifts, considered by itself, ranged from 500,000 families removed from the 1967 total of potentially poor families by interregional shifts, to 1,900,000 families removed by occupational shifts. Movement off farms, clearly overlapping occupational shifts, accounted for 700,000 families; and interindustry shifts (also overlapping occupational shifts) for 1,700,000 families.

Chapter 6

CHANGE IN INCOME REDISTRIBUTION, VIA TAXES AND TRANSFERS

INTRODUCTION

Poverty reduction is related to income inequality in a number of ways. If reduction in the number of persons in poverty proceeds at a fast enough rate relative to the rate of increase in average income, it forces a reduction in inequality of income. Similarly, a rapid filling of the poverty-income gap by whatever means, even though it may not be accompanied by a reduction in the number of persons in poverty, will lead to a larger share of total income going to the lowest fifth of income receivers, and hence in most cases a lesser degree of overall inequality.[1] In the longer run, bringing more families above the poverty line may well contribute to the ability of young people to make the kinds of changes in search of higher earned incomes which were discussed in the preceding chapter. That kind of long-run change may also follow from heavier investment in the poor by the community in the form of better education, health, and other services. This also involves a redistribution or change in income distribution to the extent that the poor do not pay for the full cost of the improved services to them.

In Part A we concluded that since the 1930s both the functional and the size distribution of income have moved toward less inequality. These moves toward less inequality of wealth and income are apparently in some part due to the workings of "the market," that is, to private responses to economic changes. They are also in some part due to government policies and responses, principally education, welfare, and health service programs which improve the ability and motivation of poor persons to compete in the marketplace. Also important are money-transfer programs. Government expenditures for these services and money transfers may be grouped under the heading of "social welfare expenditures."

---

[1]This would not be the case if the increase in the share of the lowest fifth were accomplished by a reduction in the share of the second lowest fifth.

Taxes also affect income inequality and the possibility of escaping from poverty.

In this chapter we examine historical changes in social welfare expenditures and the tax system and then look at the combined tax-transfer system.

HISTORICAL CHANGES IN SOCIAL WELFARE EXPENDITURES

According to Ida C. Merriam, social welfare expenditures in 1966–67 amounted to 13.1 percent of GNP, a far greater share than the 7.8 percent of 1946–47 (see Table 6.1). Table 6.2 shows that there have been tremendous increases in per capita social welfare expenditures since 1928. Unfortunately, we do not have a basis for good estimates of how the poor's share of these transfers may have changed over the years.

How do social welfare expenditures influence the number of persons in poverty over time? Could it be that the expenditures made ten or twenty or thirty years ago, especially those which benefited children, are responsible for the escape from poverty this year by some who are now heads of families? If this is so, we might consider the year-by-year increases in transfers lagged twenty years as explaining current and future poverty reduction.

A lagged payoff in taking people out of poverty would suggest that in the decade 1947–57 poverty reduction was furthered by the social welfare expenditures of 1928–40, which rose from $64.89 to $163.08 per capita in constant dollars (see Table 6.2). We might assume the poverty reduction of 1957–67 was responsive to social welfare expenditures of 1939–50, when per capita expenditures rose from $163.08 to $211.34. The 1949–60 increase in per capita social welfare expenditures —from $211.34 to $316.18, also in constant dollars—should contribute to poverty reduction in the 1970s.

HISTORICAL CHANGES IN THE TAX SYSTEM

Expenditures by governments are, of course, only one side of government transactions as they affect the poor. The other side is taxes, and it is at least possible that taxes could do as much to push people into, or keep them in, poverty as social welfare expenditures do to take them out

Table 6.1. Social Welfare Expenditures under Public Programs as Percent of GNP
(Selected Fiscal Years)

Fiscal year	GNP ($ billions)	Total	Social welfare expenditures as percent of GNP					
			Social insurance	Public aid	Health and medical programs	Veterans' programs	Education	Other social welfare
1889–90	13.0	2.4	—	0.3	0.1	0.9	1.1	—
1928–29	101.0	3.9	0.3	0.1	0.3	0.7	2.4	0.1
1936–37	86.5	9.1	0.6	4.0	0.6	1.0	2.7	0.1
1946–47	221.2	7.8	1.9	0.7	0.6	2.6	1.8	0.1
1956–57	431.7	9.1	2.9	0.8	0.9	1.2	3.2	0.2
1966–67	763.1	13.1	4.9	1.2	1.1	0.9	4.7	0.4

Source: Ida C. Merriam, "Social Welfare Expenditures, 1929–67," *Social Security Bulletin* (December 1967) Table 2, p. 11.

Table 6.2.   Changes in Per Capita Total Social Welfare Expenditures, in
Constant 1966–67 Prices, 1928–29 through 1966–67

Fiscal year	Per capita expenditures ($)	Average annual increase ($)	Average annual rate of increase (%)
1928–29	$ 64.89		
		$10.82	12.3
1934–35	129.80		
		6.66	4.6
1939–40	163.08		
		−9.90	−7.0
1944–45	113.59		
		19.55	13.3
1949–50	211.34		
		5.17	2.3
1954–55	237.19		
		15.80	5.9
1959–60	316.18		
		18.75	5.2
1964–65	409.95		
		43.49	10.6
1965–66	453.55		
		43.70	9.6
1966–67	497.14		

Source: Col. 1: Ida C. Merriam, "Social Welfare Expenditures, 1929–67," *Social Security Bulletin* (December 1967), Table 3, p. 12. Cols. 2 and 3 are derived from col. 1.

of poverty or reduce their poverty-income gaps. Between 1929 and 1967, when social welfare expenditures increased from 3.9 to 13.1 percent of GNP (see Table 6.1), total taxes of federal, state, and local governments increased from 11 to 28 percent of GNP (or from 13 to 35 percent of personal income: see Table 6.3).

Taxes bear on the poverty question in a number of ways. As we indicated earlier, they should be considered in the setting and in the year-to-year adjustment of the poverty line. The original setting of the line presumably takes account of the taxes in effect in the base period. To the extent that taxes raise consumer prices and depress wages, all that is needed is a cost-of-living adjustment from year to year. (However, taxes having those effects may be working against poverty reduction.) On the other hand, changes in taxes which do not raise prices or depress wage rates but simply reduce take-home pay will not be caught in a cost-of-living adjustment in the poverty line.

94

Table 6.3. Selected Data on Federal, State, and Local Taxes (Selected Years)

	1929	1939	1946	1954	1958	1960	1967
Total taxes ($ billions)	11.3	15.4	51.7	86.8	115.1	138.3	223.8
Federal ($ billions)	3.8	6.7	39.7	62.8	78.8	94.8	147.6
State and local ($ billions)	7.5	8.7	12.0	24.0	36.3	43.5	76.2
Total taxes as percent of GNP	11	17	25	24	25	27	28
Total taxes as percent of personal income	13	21	29	30	31	34	35
Specific types of taxes as percent of total taxes							
Total	100	100	100	100	100	100	100
Income taxes (individual and corporate)	23	17	51	54	52	48	46
Property taxes	41	28	10	11	11	12	12
Social insurance contributions	[a]	14	11	13	13	13	17
Sales, excise, and other taxes	36	42	28	22	24	27	25

[a] 0.2 percent.

Source: For 1929–54: Department of Commerce, *Survey of Current Business*, National Income Supplement. For 1958–67: Council of Economic Advisers, *Annual Report*.

Our interest in taxes, in this context, is in how changes in the twenty-year period under review may have contributed to, or worked against, poverty reduction. We gain some insight into this by noting that taxes have gone up absolutely and as a share of personal income. But has the tax burden on the poor increased more than the burden on the nonpoor over this period? Our answer is no, but it takes quite a bit of explaining, which we begin by a look at historical shifts in the tax structure.

Before World War I the overall combination of taxes was regressive. That is, it compounded the pretax inequality of incomes. In those days local government was the most important tax collector and the local property tax was by far the most important tax in the nation. The federal government raised its revenues almost entirely by customs duties and excises upon liquor and tobacco, while state governments relied almost entirely upon property and sales taxes. In 1909 Congress passed a corporation income tax law and started the ball rolling on the Sixteenth Amendment. This gave to the federal government the power to tax personal incomes at progressive rates. At about the same time, in 1911, Wisconsin enacted what is generally regarded as the first successful state income tax.

During World War I it was established that income taxes could yield large revenues. Although there was a retreat from heavy use of income taxes in the 1920s, income taxing did appear to be firmly established as a part of the economic policy of government (see Table 6.3). By 1929 some measure of equalization had become fixed as an outstanding characteristic of our fiscal system; indeed, this characteristic was almost as highly developed in 1929 as it is today.

It is interesting that income taxation became relatively less important in the overall tax picture during the 1930s. In 1939 only 17 percent of all taxes were levied on income as compared to 23 percent in 1929. This drop occurred even though the federal government (1) increased the top rates (few people had high incomes subject to the higher rates during the Depression years) and (2) at the same time raised rates on lower incomes and increased the number of income tax payers from 2.9 million in 1929 to 3.9 million in 1939 by lower exemptions. Also during the 1930s, the property tax was being supplemented by the somewhat more regressive sales and excise taxes at the state and local level. Employment taxes or Social Security contributions, also regressive in their effect, rose from almost zero in 1929 to over 10 percent of all taxes in 1939. Hence it is not clear that the 1930s saw any broad steps forward as far as income equalization via taxes goes. Taxes were heavier, at 17 percent of personal income, and much of the tax revenue (as well as the borrowed money) went for relief of the poor. But the tax system itself remained no more redistributive than it had been before.

In World War II taxes zoomed up to over 25 percent of personal income and have stayed there since. In this period federal taxes have had the kind of dominance held by local taxes before World War I. Over two-thirds of our tax dollars have been going to the federal government since 1942. (This ratio has been declining, however, since 1950.) Income taxes in the 1950s and 1960s raised about half of all revenue, compared to a mere 17 percent in 1939.

Income taxes have fallen in relative importance, from providing 51 percent of all revenues in 1946 to only 46 percent in 1967. This fall has been accommodated by a rise in the relative importance of social insurance contributions and sales and excise taxes, which together raised 39 percent of all revenues in the earlier year and 42 percent in 1967. The changes in tax structure since 1946 do not, on the face of things, preclude the possibility that the changes were to the disadvantage of the poor, relative to the nonpoor. To look into this possibility more closely we need first to ask how taxes in any one year alter the original inequality of income. Table 6.5 begins to answer this question. The right-hand column shows that the federal personal income tax (the largest single revenue producer, which is usually thought of as the big gun of the equalizer) does not appear to shake up the distribution by fifths very much. The top fifth received 44.9 percent of the pretax income and 43 percent of the posttax income. The share of each other fifth is changed very little. This is, in part, because the high progressive rates do not take hold until well above the minimum income of the top 5 percent of consumer units.

The marginal rates of this tax in 1963 ranged from 20 percent on the first bracket of income subject to the tax to a top rate of 91 percent. These high rates may be thought of as indicating about the outside limit of progressive taxation ever considered by the American people. Average rates, derived from dividing total tax by total *taxable* income, are, of course, lower. The average rate of tax on $100,000 of taxable income for a married taxpayer with two dependents was only 40 percent in 1964.

However, these marginal and average tax rates give a misleading picture of the degree of equalization accomplished, since they apply to only a fraction of personal income. Effective tax rates are found by calculating total tax by total *income* (rather than total taxable income). There is, of course, a big gap betwen income received by persons and that part of income which is taxable—this gap being made up of what is excluded from and deducted from income in calculating net taxable income. Since taxable income is only about 40 percent of total income, it follows that the marginal tax rates quoted also overstate the amount of tax paid as a percent of total income. The typical taxpayer with income of $100,000 actually pays something less than 30 percent of his total income in income tax. Table 6.4 shows the lowest quintile with an effective tax

Table 6.4.   Distribution of Family Personal Income before and after Federal Individual Income Tax among Quintiles and Top 5 Percent of Consumer Units, 1956

| Quintile | Lower income limit of quintile ($) | Percent distribution of family personal income | | Federal individual income tax paid as percent of income |
		Before federal individual income tax	After federal individual income tax	
Lowest	—	5.0	5.3	3.2
2	2510	11.3	11.9	5.6
3	4120	16.5	17.1	7.1
4	5660	22.3	22.7	8.8
Highest	7790	44.9	43.0	14.1
Total	—	100.0	100.0	10.2
Top 5 percent	13,500	20.1	18.0	19.7

Source: Department of Commerce, *Survey of Current Business* (April 1958), Table 10, p. 8.

rate of 3.2 percent as compared to the top 5 percent with a rate of 19.7 percent. This degree of progression is not sufficient to alter the shares of income received by the several percentage groups in any substantial manner.

A recent study by Benjamin A. Okner[2] provides quantitative measures of the actual redistribution and some potential for further redistribution via this tax. He found that the 1965 tax decreased "the area of inequality" by 17.7 percent. He also found by simulation that quite radical-sounding changes in the tax law would do relatively little to change the degree of inequality. For example, using "total income" as a tax base would reduce inequality by only 4.26 percent. It would change the share of after-tax income going to taxfilers with under $3000 by less than one-half a percentage point. However, such a change would cut the share of income going to very high-income people by about half (see Table 6.5). This illustrates very well that some tax measures that would reduce inequality would do little to reduce poverty.

---

[2]*Income Distribution and the Federal Income Tax* (Ann Arbor: Institute of Public Administration, University of Michigan, 1966).

Table 6.5. Changes in Income Distribution Associated with Hypothetical Changes in Income Tax Law

Change in tax law	Percentage increase or decrease in after-1965 tax area of inequality	Share of after-tax income of tax filing units	
		Under $3000	$500,000 and over
Abolish income tax	+17.70%	7.694%	[a]
Change to flat rate of 19 percent	+ 1.83	8.072	0.707%
Abolish personal exemptions	+ 1.12	8.031	.609
1964 Revenue Act	0.00	8.158	.579
Return to 1963 tax law	– 0.05	8.204	.581
Disallow all nonbusiness deduction	– 1.11	8.501	.577
Abolish all exclusions	– 1.47	8.292	.366
Eliminate income splitting	– 1.67	8.294	.585
Use total income as tax base	– 4.26	8.411	0.286

[a]Not available.

Sources: Col. 1: text tables and derivations from data cited in text of Benjamin A. Okner, *Income Distribution* (Ann Arbor: Institute of Public Administration, University of Michigan, 1966). Cols. 2 and 3: appendix tables E-1 through E-5, ibid.

Aside from the federal individual income tax, the only other substantial tax in the American system believed to have a progressive effect is the corporate income tax. Assuming that two-thirds of this tax is borne by the stockholders, and allocating the tax to the income groups known to own most of the stock, it has been estimated by Richard A. Musgrave that this tax has a proportional effect, with rates of around 4 percent, up to $10,000 of income and then has a sharply progressive effect, with a rate of 14 percent for the over $10,000 bracket.[3] According to this estimate, the corporate income tax is the most equalizing of all taxes and plays a big role in determining the overall pattern of taxes. This follows from the fact that ownership of corporate stock is so highly concentrated.

It should be emphasized that this conclusion about progressivity is based upon a critical assumption that the tax reduces corporate profits but has little influence upon prices paid by the consumer. There is con- *X* siderable controversy among economists whether this tax is in fact paid by stockholders. A good case can be made that, particularly in a period of inflationary pressure, corporations are able to pass on a considerable part of the tax to consumers in the form of higher prices and to maintain their earlier rates of posttax profits. Another part of the tangled argument is that those who buy stocks after the tax is imposed may buy free of the tax by paying only an amount equal to the capitalized value of earnings per share after the corporate tax. It is perhaps safe to say here that by assuming that most of the tax is borne by stockholders, we have overstated the progressivity of this tax.

The personal and corporate income taxes levied by the federal government, then, supply the major progressive elements in the overall tax system. All the other federal taxes and the state and local taxes taken together have a regressive effect which tempers the progressivity of the federal income taxes. The regressive part of the system is largely made up of sales and excise taxes (which yield two-thirds of state revenues) and property taxes (which produce nine-tenths of local revenues). Social Security contributions also add to regressivity. It is assumed that these regressive taxes are shifted in the form of higher prices or rents or result in lower wages and hence take a larger part of the income of the poor than of the rich, since both consumption expenditures and wages are a larger part of the incomes of the poor than of the rich. Considering all taxes together, Musgrave found a smooth rise in the percentage that taxes

---

[3]"The Incidence of the Tax Structure and Its Effects on Consumption," Federal Tax Policy for Economic Growth and Stability (papers submitted by panelists appearing before the Subcommittee on Tax Policy, Joint Committee on the Economic Report, November 9, 1955).

were of incomes in 1954, ranging from 27 percent of income for the under $2,000 bracket to 41 percent for the over $10,000 bracket.[4]

We have adjusted Musgrave's estimates of the overall pattern of taxes for 1954 to show the effective rates by quintiles (see Table 6.6).

Table 6.6. Distribution of Family Personal Income before and after All Taxes among Fifths and the Top 5 Percent of Consumer Units (1954)

| Fifths | Mean amount of family personal income ($) | All taxes paid as percent of income | Percent distribution of | |
			Family personal income	After-tax income
Lowest	1289	24	4.8	5.3
2	2975	26	11.1	11.9
3	4401	27	16.4	17.3
4	6019	28	22.5	23.4
Highest	12,096	36	45.2	41.8
Total	5356	31	100.0	100.0
Top 5 percent	21,761	42	20.3	17.0

Working with these rates, we are able to suggest how the overall pattern of inequality was altered by taxes. The income share of the lowest quintile was raised from 4.8 to 5.3 percent while the share of the top quintile was dropped 3.4 percentage points. The pretax share of the top 5 percent was cut 3.3 percentage points, or 16 percent of the way toward zero, by taxes.

COMPARATIVE VIEW OF INCOME EQUALIZATION BY TAXES, 1938–65

It is possible to compare the overall tax rates picture of 1954 with two earlier periods and two later periods, since similar studies have been made for 1938–39, 1946–47, 1948, and 1965. Roughly similar methods were followed by the scholars who made the estimates: Helen Tarasov,

---

[4]Ibid. More precisely, these rates are calculated by dividing total taxes allocated to income brackets by total income in the bracket adjusted to include realized capital gains, undistributed corporate profits, and other items. There are, of course, some difficulties in relating these tax rates back to personal income, but it is not believed that they are so serious as to vitiate the comparisons made.

John H. Adler,[5] Musgrave, and the Council of Economic Advisers. Such a comparison presents many puzzling problems, since everything moves over time, including the level of taxes, the pattern of taxes, the number of people in each income bracket, and the general level of prices and incomes.

Since we are interested in relating the tax structure to income inequality, it is useful to get around some of these problems by showing the rates by fifths of income receivers (see Table 6.7). Prosperity and inflation have, of course, changed the income limits of the several quintiles very considerably in the last thirty years. The highest fifth began at $2420 in 1939 and at $11,000 in 1965 (all figures are in current dollars). The postwar rates are, of course, markedly higher, but all four rate schedules show a progressive slant. The 1954 rate schedule appears from casual inspection to be more progressive than the prewar schedules, and this is confirmed by calculations (not given here) which show that while the actual 1954 rates dropped the share of pretax personal income of the top fifth of consumer units from 45.2 to 41.8 percent, application of 1938 rates would have resulted in a lesser drop, to 43.9 percent. The result of 1948 rates would have been intermediate between the results of 1938–39 and 1954.

The broad conclusion that may be drawn from these tables is that there is some, but not a striking difference between the equalizing effects of the overall tax system which existed in the 1950s and 1960s and the effects of the system which existed in the 1930s and the late 1940s. The American tax system is, and has been for some decades, a mildly equalizing one. It results in the poor having a slightly larger share of post-tax income than it has of pretax income.[6] We started this section with the question: Has the tax burden on the poor increased more than the burden on the nonpoor in recent years? Our answer to that question is no.

It must be admitted that this conclusion is based upon what is necessarily a crude comparison over time. In some regards this comparison tends to understate the increase in equalizing effect; in others it tends to overstate it. Perhaps the most important change in recent years which is not accounted for is change in family size by income level. Since the

---

[5]The estimates for 1938–39 and 1946–47 are brought together by Adler in his paper on "The Fiscal System, the Distribution of Income, and Public Welfare," in Kenyon Poole, ed., *Fiscal Policies and the American Economy* (Englewood Cliffs, N.J.: Prentice-Hall, 1951).

[6]For a discouraging account of the barriers in the way of a more redistributive tax system, see Joseph A. Pechman, "The Rich, the Poor, and the Taxes They Pay," *The Public Interest*, No. 17 (Fall 1969), pp. 21–43.

Table 6.7. Percent of Personal Income Taken by Federal, State, and Local Taxes from Each Fifth and Top 5 Percent of Consumer Units (Selected Years)

Fifth of consumer units	1938–39		1948		1954		1965[a]	
	Lower income limit of quintile ($)	All taxes as percent of income	Lower income limit of quintile ($)	All taxes as percent of income	Lower income limit of quintile ($)	All taxes as percent of income	Lower income limit of quintile ($)	All taxes, as percent of income
Lowest	—	19	—	26	—	24	—	22
2	650	18	1760	25	2200	26	3300	24
3	1150	18	2900	26	3700	27	5500	25
4	1730	18	3930	26	5120	28	7600	26
Highest	2420	22	5650	32	7100	36	11,000	33
Total	—	20	—	29	—	31	—	29
Top 5 percent	4460	25	9800	38	12,350	42	18,000	42

[a]Council of Economic Advisers, Mimeographed Memorandum released as background to 1969 *Annual Report*, p. 161. Adapted to show taxes as percent of posttransfer income.

Depression, size of consumer unit has come to be more directly associated with income—that is, lower-income units are more typically smaller families than used to be the case (see Table 4.5). This means that in the comparison over time it is plausible to say that the high tax rates at the top of the income range now apply to relatively more persons than did the comparable rates in 1938 or 1948, that is, there has been more increase in progressivity on a *per person* basis than on a per consumer unit basis. It is worth a comment here that all of the foregoing calculations show taxes paid by income bracket. A better breakdown would first make an adjustment for family size and then show taxes paid by the *poor* versus taxes paid by the *nonpoor*. Since not all those with income below $2000 or $3000 are poor, according to the Social Security Administration, and some with incomes above $3000 *are* poor, the redistributive effects of taxes toward the poor are imperfectly shown. No one has yet done a complete study of taxes paid by families in the poor-nonpoor categories, although some fragmentary estimates are provided by Morgan et al., and Bridges.[7] The latter estimates are used in the following discussion of transfers and taxes to pay for them.

A SYSTEM OF PRIVATE
AND PUBLIC TRANSFERS

Earlier it was mentioned that social welfare expenditures play an important role in poverty reduction. However, it is important to note that those expenditures are only part of a highly developed system of private as well as public, and nonmoney as well as money, transfers. By adding up all these transfers and estimating the share which goes to the poor, and by accounting for the taxes and contributions paid by the poor, we can get some impression of the role that transfers, both positive and negative, play in reducing poverty.

In this section we use the term "transfer" to mean a receipt of either money or a good or service for which less than a full quid pro quo payment was made, or service delivered, by the recipient in the current period.

---

[7]James Morgan, Martin David, Wilbur J. Cohen, and Harvey Brazer, *Income and Welfare in the United States* (New York: McGraw-Hill, 1962); U.S. Congress, Joint Economic Committee, "Current Redistributional Effects of Old Age Assurance Programs" (Old Age Income Assurance, Part II), prepared by Benjamin Bridges, Jr. (Washington, D.C.: U.S. Government Printing Office, 1967).

We may picture the several institutions[8] that are involved in redistribution, or alternatively, the conversion of producer income to consumer income, by reference to Figure 6.1. Factor incomes flow out of the productive process toward the suppliers of labor and property. The first stage at which redistribution may be said to occur is that of subsidy to raise certain factor incomes (an example of this would be a wage subsidy). The second is at the employer level (and this should include the public as well as the private employer) when he diverts what would otherwise be factor income to cover pooled risks of employees. The third is tax payments to public agencies to provide for cash and in-kind transfers and subsidies. We are not including all taxes and all government expenditures. Only the quantity of taxes needed to pay for what may be considered "personally received" transfers is included. Our guide for inclusion for the latter is Ida C. Merriam's "social welfare expenditures under public programs" series.[9] The fourth is when factor income is appropriated by the earner to the financial intermediary for insurance purposes. A fifth is a subsidy to lower the market price of a consumer good. Sixth, transfers are made by families and business enterprises via private philanthropic institutions. Seventh, transfers are made directly on an interfamily basis, and to secondary units. (We exclude all transfers within primary family units.) In all these cases some persons are receiving consumer-power income on some basis other than their own individual producer-contribution in the current period; they are, in other words, receiving transfers. These transfers are seen as moving among several sectors: the employment, the governmental, the philanthropic, the private insurance, and the family sectors, and also within the family sector.

A rough estimate of the quantities involved in the various types of transferring in the United States in fiscal 1967 is shown in Table 6.8. The gross amounts of $132 billion worth of transfers are over one-sixth of GNP. The largest part of the transferring is done by public agencies, but a not insignificant amount is done by employers and employees via insurance benefits.[10] Philanthropic institutions play a relatively small role

---

[8]We are not accounting for such nonexpenditure measures aimed at direct change of factor incomes as minimum wage legislation, immigration laws, and prevention of racial discrimination in employment.

[9]"Social Welfare Expenditures, 1929–67," *Social Security Bulletin* (December 1967), pp. 3–16. Admittedly, the line between such expenditures and others is hard to draw.

[10]In this table public employee retirement plans are classified in item 3.

Figure 6.1.   Income generation, distribution, and redistribution

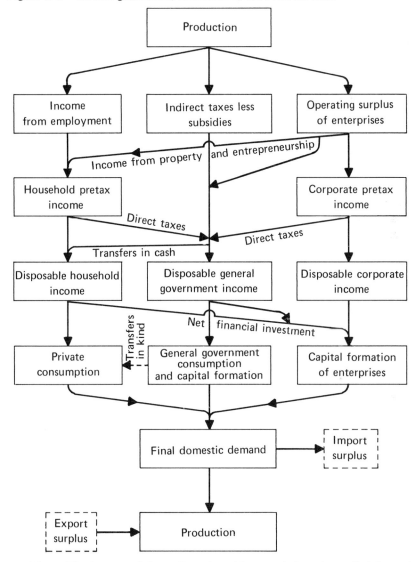

Note: The income of the self-employed is regarded as channelled from the operating surplus of enterprises at the top of the chart, into household income. Capital formation by households, including self-employers, is channelled back from household income to capital formation in the lower part of the chart.

Source: United Nations, Secretariat of the Economic Commission for Europe, *Incomes in Post-war Europe: A Study of Policies, Growth and Distribution* (Geneva, 1967), p. 2.

Table 6.8. Components of American System of Transfers (Fiscal 1967)

Item	Family receipts ($ billions)	Family payments ($ billions)
Increase in factor income due to subsidy	1	(see line 3)
Employer-financed privately insured benefits	7	7
Tax-financed public cash and in-kind transfers	100	102 (sum of lines 1, 3, and 5)
Employee-financed group and individual private insurance benefits	10	10
Reduction in market price due to subsidy	1	(see line 3)
Transfers via philanthropic institutions	3	3
Interfamily transfers	10	10
Total	132	132

compared to interfamily transfers. As we noted earlier, intrafamily transfers among members of a single primary family are not estimated.

Perhaps it is unnecessary to point out that the types of transfers discussed are to a certain extent substitutes for one another. The same purpose of income redistribution may sometimes be accomplished alternatively by subsidy at the factor payment level, or by a tax reduction, or by cash transfer at the family level. Public programs may replace private ones, or private transferring may be made compulsory. Over time, a national economy may evolve a new balance among these several institutions, and this balance may be referred to as the system of transfers. This new balance may be arrived at with or without an increase in the share of factor income which is redistributed.[11]

Historically, at least, the insurance device and the public transfer programs have risen to serve in part as substitutes for the declining importance of the extended family as a redistributor. Similarly, public programs have taken over in problem areas that were at one time largely the domain of private philanthropy. However, the separate parts of the tax structure, of Social Security, and of collective consumption have been developed quite independently. They have rarely been regarded as interrelated parts of a coherent system of redistribtuion. Therefore, to many

[11]Cf. Robert J. Lampman, "The Effectiveness of Some Institutions in Changing the Distribution of Income," *American Economic Review* 47 (May 1957), 519–28.

practical people it will seem artificial and unhelpful to isolate and summarize the redistributive effects of numerous programs having heteroge-
neous purposes and addressed to separate parts of the population. Not
only does it take a great effort of the imagination to conceive of the patch-
work we now have as a system, it also seems to suggest that there should
be a central decisionmaking committee on these matters. Such a committee does not, of course, exist in this country. Moreover, there is no
common pool of funds out of which the whole range of programs is
financed, and hence an increase in funds for one program is not necessarily at the expense of a forgone increase in another. Nonetheless, it is
sensible to ask whether we are getting the most possible social advantage
from the present $132 billion and more of transfers. That question calls
for a new discipline of "the economics of health, education, and welfare." This special branch of economics—concerned with the allocations
of resources to medical care and schooling and the redistribution of income by cash transfers—would have a certain unity because the reallo-
cations in the fields of health and education are intended to have redistributive effects, and the cash payments have reallocative effects.
This means that it is hard to separate allocative efficiency from distributional equity. It is also true that in all three areas there is an unusual mix
of private and public suppliers, a complex structure of demand, probabi-
listic events, unusually uncertain outcomes, and extraordinarily significant external benefits.

The Poor's Share of Total Transfers

Table 6.9 offers a rough estimate of how the $132 billion of total
transfers (including money and in-kind and public and private transfer)
are shared and paid for as between the pretransfer poor and the nonpoor.
The dividing lines between poor and nonpoor are those set out by the
Social Security Administration for families of various sizes. The pretransfer poor were 25 percent and the posttransfer poor were 15 percent
of the total population. The allocations made in Table 6.9 are "back of
the envelope" calculations made from fragmentary information, some of
which is based on the years 1959–61; hence the specific numbers should
not be taken as any more than rough approximations. Allocations for
items 3a, 3b, and 3c are based on the 1966–67 Survey of Economic
Opportunity data reported in the next section. The allocation for 3f,
which is based on the work of Morgan et al., assumes that the pretransfer
poor get 25 percent of the benefit of expenditures for primary and

secondary education and 10 percent of higher education benefits.[12] Item 3, taxes, is based upon an assumed proportional tax sufficient to raise $102 billion. Since the pretransfer poor have 9 percent of post-transfer money income, they are assigned 9 percent of the taxes.

According to these rough estimates, the pretransfer poor in 1967 received $49.2 billion in transfers, about half of which came to them in the form of public assistance and social insurance.[13] In return, they contributed $10.7 billion through private and public channels. Their net gain was, then, $38.5 billions, which was more than their original factor income of $20 billion. This gain was at the expense of the nonpoor who received $82.8 billion and paid $121.3 billion. The whole array of public and private givings and takings raised the share of pretransfer poor families from 3 percent of pre-redistribution income to 9 percent of post-redistribution income. This was accomplished by public transfers (positive and negative) and distributional allocations, which raised the share from 3 to 8 percent; and by private transfers and allocations, which raised it to 9 percent. This gain in share was accomplished by an off-setting decline in share of income on the part of the pretransfer nonpoor families.[14]

The Poor's Share of Money Transfers

Cash income maintenance benefits are the only public expenditures, other than "direct subsidies to increase factor incomes" which immediately enter into total money income, and since the poverty line is stated in terms of pre-income tax total money income, they would seem to have unique relevance out of all the items listed in Table 6.9 to the question of poverty reduction. It does seem ironic that cash benefits went up from under $25 billion in 1959 to almost $43 billion in 1967 (see column 3 of Table 6.10) while the poverty-income gap fell only from $13.7 billion to

---

[12]Morgan et al., *Income and Welfare in the United States*, p. 304, Table 19–13.

[13]Cf. Michael S. March, "Public Programs for the Poor: Coverage, Gaps, and Future Directions," *Federal Programs for the Development of Human Resources*, Vol. I, U.S. Congress, Joint Economic Committee, 1968, Appendix A, pp. 143–53. He estimates that the federal government spent $25.6 billion in "assisting the poor" in 1968. This is up from $9.9 billion in 1960. The 1968 funds went to cash transfers in the amount of $14.6 billion; education and training, $3.8 billion; health, $4.2 billion; and other services, $3.1 billion. Additionally, state and local governments spent $12.9 billion and private voluntary agencies spent $2.4 billion, to make up a total of $40 billion for the poor (ibid., Table 3).

[14]These calculations are discussed more fully in Robert J. Lampman, "Transfer Approaches to Distribution Policy," *American Economic Review* 60 (May 1970), 270–79.

Table 6.9. Pretransfer Poor's Share of Transfers (Fiscal 1967)

Item	Total ($ billions)	Share of pretransfer poor in			
		Family receipts		Family payments	
		Percent	Amount ($ billions)	Percent	Amount ($ billions)
1. Increase in factor income due to subsidy	1	10	0.1	—	(see line 3)
2. Employer-financed insured benefits	7	5	0.4	3	0.2
3. Tax-financed public cash and in-kind transfers and subsidies	100	42	42.1	9	9.2 (includes lines 1 and 5)
a. Social insurance benefits	37	50	18.5		
b. Public aid benefits	9	93	8.4		
c. Veterans' benefits	7	46	3.2		
d. Other welfare services and public housing	3	50	1.5		
e. Health benefits	8	50	4.0		
f. Education benefits	36	18	6.5		
4. Employee-financed insurance benefits	10	5	0.5	3	0.3
5. Reduction in market price due to subsidy	1	10	0.1	—	(see line 3)
6. Transfer via philanthropic institutions	3	33	1.0	5	0.2
a. Health benefits	1	50	0.1	—	—
b. Education benefits	2	20	0.4	—	—
c. Other welfare benefits	1	50	0.5	—	—
7. Interfamily transfers	10	50	5.0	5	0.8
8. Total	132	37	49.2	8	10.7

Table 6.10. Social Welfare Expenditures under Public Programs (Selected Years)

Year	All social welfare expenditures ($ billions)	Noncash benefits ($ billions)	Cash benefits under public income maintenance programs ($ billions)					
			Total	Retirement Disability and Survivors	Unemployment	Temporary Disability	Workmen's Compensation	Public Assistance
1940	8.8	4.6	4.2	0.8	0.5	—	0.2	1.0
1950	23.5	14.8	8.7	4.3	1.5	0.1	0.4	2.4
1960	52.3	26.4	25.9	8.2	3.0	0.4	0.9	3.3
1963	66.8	34.4	32.4	24.1	2.9	0.4	1.1	3.6
1967	99.7	57.1	42.6	33.4	2.4	0.5	1.4	4.9
1968	112.0	63.8	48.2	38.0	2.4	0.5	1.6	5.7
1969	126.8							
1970	143.0							

Source: Col. 1: Ida C. Merriam, Alfred M. Skolnick, and Sophie R. Dales, "Social Welfare Expenditures, 1967–68," *Social Security Bulletin* (December 1968), pp. 14–27. For 1969 and 1970: *Social Security Bulletin* (December 1970), Table 1, p. 4. All other cols.: *Social Security Bulletin* (September 1969), Table M–1, p. 33.

$9.7 billion. This suggests that the increases in money transfers have been directed in large part at the pretransfer nonpoor.

We do not have a good series on the number of pretransfer poor, but it does appear that transfers have been taking increasing numbers of households to posttransfer incomes above the poverty line. We found, using 1961 Bureau of Labor Statistics Consumer Expenditure Survey data, that transfers took 4.7 million households out of poverty in that year.[15] This is the same number counted by Mollie Orshansky with regard to government transfers only for 1965.[16] Irene Lurie found that transfers took 6.1 million households out of poverty in 1966,[17] and we confirm that number by an independent computation of recently available data collected by the Survey of Economic Opportunity.[18] This survey enables us to know more than ever before about who receives the several types of public and private transfers listed in Table 6.11. The total amount of these transfers recorded for 1966 was $39.2 billion, which was 8.5 percent of the total family money income there recorded of $462.1 billion. Out of all the families and unrelated individuals in the nation, 24.9 million, or 40 percent of the total, received a transfer (see Table 6.12). (Hereafter in this section, the term "families" includes unrelated individuals. This definition corresponds to the "interview unit" in the SEO files. The poor are defined here as those with incomes below the Social Security Administration guidelines.)

These transfers had great impact on the pretransfer poor families, who numbered 16.1 million in 1966. This group had a mean pretransfer poverty-income gap of $1500; 12.3 million of these families received a transfer, the mean amount of which was $1840 per recipient; and 6.1 million families were taken out of poverty by transfers. After transfers,

        [15]Robert J. Lampman, "How Much Does the American System of Transfers Benefit the Poor?"

        [16]Mollie Orshansky, "The Shape of Poverty in 1966," *Social Security Bulletin* (March 1968), pp. 3–32.

        [17]Irene Lurie, "Transfer Payments and Income Maintenance," mimeographed Staff Paper for the President's Commission on Income Maintenance Programs (1969).

        [18]U.S. Bureau of the Census, Survey of Economic Opportunity, 1966 and 1967. This survey, which was sponsored by the Office of Economic Opportunity, was carried out by the Bureau of the Census. A tape prepared by the Brookings Institution was released to research agencies, including the Institute for Research on Poverty, in August 1969. The results reported here are the first computed from that tape by the staff of the Institute with the assistance of the Data and Computation Center of the Social Systems Research Institute of the University of Wisconsin. No attempts have been made to correct for underreporting. Further, no study has yet been made by the author of possible inconsistencies between these data and those from other sources.

Table 6.11. Number of Families Receiving Transfers and Mean Amount of Those Transfers

Item	Pretransfer poor families		Pretransfer nonpoor families		All families	
	Number (thousands)	Mean ($)	Number (thousands)	Mean ($)	Number (thousands)	Mean ($)
All transfers	12,260	1840	12,651	1310	24,911	1570
Social Security	8846	1280	5248	1170	14,094	1240
Government pensions	1382	1790	1236	2250	2619	2010
Veterans' pensions	1518	1040	1842	820	3360	920
Private pensions	1195	1300	793	1400	1988	1340
Workmen's Compensation	315	1050	1713	410	2028	510
Unemployment Insurance	459	510	2408	380	2867	400
Public Assistance	2660	1170	567	760	3228	1100
Other transfers[a]	1329	1510	1899	1600	3228	1570

[a]Includes the following items: (1) money contributions received periodically from persons not living in the household, such as payments received by parents from children not living with them; (2) benefits paid by private welfare groups (Public Assistance and lump-sum payments are not included); (3) periodic payments from life insurance policies of a deceased person; (4) alimony received periodically after a divorce or legal separation; (5) money received from oil, gas, or other mineral rights, from timber royalties, as well as periodic payments from patents, copyrights, and trademarks.

Table 6.12. Total Money Transfers Received by Families and Effects of These Transfers on Family Poverty Status (1966)

	Number of families (millions)	Total transfers received ($ billions)	Total poverty-income gap	
			Pretransfer ($ billions)	Posttransfer ($ billions)
All families	61.7	39.2	—	—
Pretransfer nonpoor	45.6	16.6	—	—
Pretransfer poor	16.1	22.6	24.3	1.7
Taken out of poverty by transfers	6.1	15.8	7.8	−8.0
Posttransfer poor	10.0	6.8	16.5	9.7

	Number of families (millions)	Mean transfers received ($)	Mean poverty-income gap	
			Pretransfer ($)	Posttransfer ($)
All families	61.7	640	—	—
Pretransfer nonpoor	45.6	360	—	—
Pretransfer poor	16.1	1400	1500	106
Taken out of poverty by transfers	6.1	2590	1280	−1310
Posttransfer poor	10.0	680	1650	970

10.0 million families remained poor, but this group had a mean poverty-income gap of only $970, after transfers.

The pretransfer poverty-income gap total was $24.3 billion; post-transfer, the gap was $9.7 billion. Of $39.2 billion in total transfers, $22.6 billion went to the pretransfer poor. Of the latter amount, the greater part went to those who were taken out of poverty, or kept out of poverty, by the transfer; only $6.8 billion went to the 10 million families who remained poor after transfer.

Table 6.13 affords another look at the effect of money transfers, as

Table 6.13.   Number of Families, Mean Pretransfer Income, and Mean Amount of Transfer, by Pretransfer Welfare Ratio (1966)

Pretransfer welfare ratio[a]	Number of families (thousands)	Mean pretransfer income ($)	Mean transfer ($)
Negative	212	−1390	750
0	4266	30	1620
0−.25	4021	240	1840
.25−.50	2666	900	1330
.50−.75	2422	1660	1070
.75−1.0	2517	2530	760
1.0−1.25	2809	3570	700
1.25−1.50	2866	4460	560
1.5−2.0	6998	5620	370
2.0−3.0	12,755	7430	340
Over 3.0	20,136	12,530	300
Total	61,717	6850	640

[a]Poverty line = 1.0.

it shows how transfers changed the mean incomes of those in the several pretransfer welfare-ratio groupings.[19] While the mean income was raised by $640 for all families, it was raised by successively larger amounts for those in the lower welfare-ratio groupings but above zero. This pronouncedly pro-poor effect is undoubtedly the most striking to be observed relative to these transfers.

As we mentioned earlier, 6.1 million families were taken out of poverty by transfers in 1966. However, it is interesting to note that the group thus taken out is not representative of those who were poor before

---

[19]A family with an income at the poverty line has a welfare ratio of 1.0. A welfare ratio of 0.5 means that the family has an income one-half the poverty line for its family size.

transfer (see Table 6.14). The groups which appear to be most favored include the aged and the family heads who worked very little. By contrast,

Table 6.14. Percentage of Pretransfer Poor Families and Percentages of Families Taken Out of Poverty by Transfer, by Selected Characteristics (1966)

Characteristic	Pretransfer poor families (%)	Families taken out of poverty by transfer (%)
Family head 65 or over	50	70
Principal earner worked no more than 13 weeks during the year	61	69
Family resides in central city or urban fringe of SMSA	55	61
Family head has no more than 8 grades of schooling completed	58	56
Family head is female	44	35
Family resides in South	36	27
Family head is nonwhite	18	8
Family has 3 or more members	31	19

the least favored groups include nonwhites, who make up 18 percent of pretransfer poor families but only 8 percent of those taken out of poverty, families headed by women, families of three or more persons, and families in the South.

By use of other tabulations not reproduced here,[20] we can pursue the extent of these apparent biases; first, by looking at the frequency of receipt of transfer and the mean amount of transfer by color and by sex of family head. Nonwhites have a lower mean transfer than whites. They receive lower mean amounts than do whites of each of the several types of transfers, except for public assistance. They received a little less than 10 percent of the total amount of transfers. Transfers fill a smaller share of the poverty-income gap for nonwhites than for whites within welfare-ratio groupings. This bias is no doubt partly explained by nonwhites being disproportionately employed in occupations and firms not covered by social insurance and by their concentration in the South, where assistance benefits are relatively low.

---

[20]They are to be found in Kenneth Boulding and Martin Pfaff (eds.), *Redistribution to the Rich and the Poor* (Belmont, Calif.: Wadsworth Publishing Co., forthcoming).

Female heads have a higher mean transfer than male and receive 31 percent of the total. Families headed by women have a larger share of the poverty-income gap filled by transfers, on the average, than do families headed by men. However, this is not true for many of the lowest welfare-ratio groupings.

We turn next to the important question of how transfers relate to family size. Relatively few large families are taken out of poverty by transfers.[21] While families of three or more persons made up 31 percent of the pretransfer poor, they were only 19 percent of the families taken out of poverty. Except for families of one person, the share of the poverty-income gap filled by transfers declines, on the average, as family size increases. For families of eight or more persons, only 42 percent of the poverty-income gap was filled by transfer. Transfers vary by family size within welfare-ratio groupings but do not appear to be responsive to the needs of larger families.

The amounts transferred increase with age, from a low of $190 for those under 25 to a high average of $1680 for those heads 65 or older. This transfer pattern does not appear to be responsive to the relatively great need of families headed by persons under age 25.

Weeks worked by the principal earner vary inversely with the share of the poverty-income gap filled by transfers. Over 100 percent of the gap is filled, on the average, for those poor families whose principal earners work no more than thirteen weeks in the year; but only 60 percent of the gap is filled for poor families whose principal earners worked forty or more weeks. Transfers are not responsive to the greater poverty-income gap of families in rural areas and the South.

Table 6.15 offers more information regarding the biases in the system of cash transfers.[22] Column 1 shows the differences in the mean amounts of transfers actually received by different groups of families. For example, families with heads under 25 years of age received $190 in cash transfers per year, on the average, while families whose head is 65 years or older received a mean amount of $1680 per year. Thus the (unadjusted) deviation from the mean for *all* families ($640) for the "under 25" group is −$450, while the (unadjusted) deviation for the "65 and older" group is +$1040. In other words families in the "under 25" group actually receive $450 less in cash transfers per year, on the average, than do all families, while families in the "65 and older" group actually receive $1040

---

[21]We were able to derive considerable information on this relationship from the Survey of Consumer Expenditures of 1961. Those findings are reported in Robert J. Lampman, "How Much Does the American System of Transfers Benefit the Poor?"

[22]Table 6.15 and 6.16 are the work of Benton P. Gillingham.

Table 6.15. Characteristics Explaining the Total Amount of Money Transfer Received by All Families (Recipients and Nonrecipients) (1966) (Deviations shown are from a mean transfer of $640 per family)

Characteristic	Unadjusted deviations ($) (1)	Adjusted deviations ($) (2)	Characteristic	Unadjusted deviations ($) (1)	Adjusted deviations ($) (2)
Age of head			Weeks worked by head (Armed Forces excluded)		
Less than 25	−450	−342[a]	0–13	+1217	+771[a]
25−34	−365	−184[a]	14−26	+259	$47[a]
35−54	−271	−66[a]	27−39	−4	+20[a]
55−64	+20	+25[a]	40−52	−398	−280[a]
65 and over	+1040	+445[a]	Region		
Race			Northeast	+80	+49
White	+9	+28	North central	−53	+11
Nonwhite	−75	−51	South	−13	−45
Sex of head			West	−6	+30
Male	−85	+9	Extent of urbanization		
Female	+326	−29	Central city, in SMSA	+23	+30[a]
Family size			Urban fringe, in SMSA	−84	+55[a]
1	0	−423[a]	Urban, outside SMSA	+138	+48[b]
2	+354	+123[b]	Rural, outside SMSA	+4	−157[b]
3−4	−146	+79[a]	Pretransfer welfare ratio		
5−6	−258	+49[a]	Negative	+110	+610[b]
Over 6	−97	+332[a]	0	+984	+235[a]
Grades completed by head			0−.5	+1004	+339[a]
0−8	+233	−139[a]	.5−1.0	+279	+66[b]
9−12	−126	+50[a]	1.0−1.5	−5	−40
13−16	−154	+125[a]	1.5−2.0	−265	−64
Over 16	+215	+349[a]	2.0−3.0	−292	−136[b]
			Over 3.0	−334	−142[b]

Results of a t-test:
[a] Deviations significantly different from zero at the 1 percent level.
[b] Deviations significantly different from zero at the 5 percent level.

more, on the average, than all families. The rest of column 1 contains the unadjusted deviations for eight other family characteristics.

By looking at column 2 we gain further insight into the nature of the biases in the system of cash transfers. By using a multivariate regression analysis, we estimate the effect of each characteristic on the mean amount of cash transfers received, all other characteristics remaining the same.[23] For example, a family head's being in the lowest education group, by itself, reduces the amount of transfers received by $139.

From these more refined calculations (i.e., the adjusted deviations), we may interpret the figures in column 1 (i.e., the unadjusted deviations). Still using education as an example, we see that families with heads in the lowest education group actually receive $233 *more* in cash transfers than all families, on the average, even though the lowest education position by itself reduces the amount of cash transfers received by $139. Thus a correct inference to be drawn from this finding is that even though the lowest education group actually receives $233 more than all families, on the average, this difference is not accounted for by the lowest education position itself, but rather by other characteristics of families in this position. For another example, we find that the apparent biases against non-whites and men do not appear significant after variations in all other characteristics have been accounted for. (Note that the adjusted deviations are not significant at the 5 percent level.) On the other hand, the bias against full-year workers emerges unscathed from the regression analysis.

Using column 2, we can estimate the expected amount of transfers to be received by groups of families having any stated set of characteristics. Table 6.16 indicates that families with one particular set of characteristics will receive a mean amount of cash transfers of $404 per year, a figure which is $236 below the national average.

SUMMARY

Poverty reduction comes about through changes in composition of the population, through moves people make in search of higher incomes, and through change in income redistribution. Social welfare expenditures have increased markedly in recent decades and now amount to 13.1 percent of GNP. Poverty reduction in the 1970s may respond to the great increases in social welfare expenditures in the 1950s.

---

[23]For an explanation of this regression technique, which uses a set of "dummy" variables for each characteristic, see Morgan et al., *Income and Welfare in the United States.*

Table 6.16. Predicted Mean Transfer for Families Having a Stated Set
of Characteristics

Characteristic	Adjusted deviations from a grand mean of $640 ($)	
Family size: 3	+ 79	
Race: white	+ 0[a]	
Sex of head: male	+ 0[a]	
Age of head: 45		− 66
Education of head: 16 years	+125	
Weeks worked by head in 1966: 52		−280
Region of residence: West	+ 0[a]	
Extent of urbanization: urban, outside SMSA	+ 48	
Pretransfer welfare ratio: over 3.0		−142
Totals	+252	−488
Total adjusted deviation	252 − 488 = −236	
Expected total transfers for this family	640 − 236 = 404	

[a] These adjusted deviations were found not significantly different from zero
at the 5 percent level.
Source: Derived from col. 2 of Table 6.15.

The American tax system bears heavily on the poor as well as on
the nonpoor, but leaves the poor with a somewhat larger share of income posttaxes than it receives pretaxes. The overall progressivity of
the combined federal, state, and local taxes does not seem to have
changed very much in recent decades. On the other hand, the system
of private and public transfers is pronouncedly pro-poor in its distributive effects and yielded a benefit in 1967, net of taxes and contributions
paid, of about $38 billion to the pretransfer poor. The money transfers
alone take some 10 percent of the population out of poverty and reduce
the poverty-income gap by over $10 billion. These transfers are biased
against some groups in poverty, most notably children and the working poor.

The distribution of money transfers by family size reflects a well-
known characteristic of the American transfer payments system, namely
its emphasis upon the aged. Neither social insurance nor public assistance is designed to reach people simply because they are poor. As
Commissioner Robert M. Ball puts it:

In fact, Social Security's contribution to the solution of the problem of poverty is in considerable part a by-product of doing much more—supplying a base on which practically everyone now builds income security—the low-income and middle-income groups and the rich alike.[24]

And, in 1960, according to the Advisory Council on Public Assistance,

uncounted numbers of financially needy families and individuals still can get little or no public assistance help. They may fall between categories of the four federally-aided programs, and hence be ineligible for any of them. They may not, because of limited education or job skills or discrimination, be able to earn enough to live decently or healthfully, yet because they are employed or employable, be debarred from recourse to tax-supported assistance.[25]

With the foregoing in mind, Michael S. March concludes that

mere increase of benefit levels in present programs is likely to channel only a fraction of the benefit dollar to the poor. If we relied on this approach to close the $11.5 billion gap without modifying present programs, we could not do so even if we doubled the present $36 billion annual outlay, because millions who need help would not be reached inasmuch as they are today excluded by laws and regulations.[26]

He estimates that "one-half or even two-thirds of the 15 million children in poverty live in poor families that receive no benefits" and laments that "our society seemingly lacks the ingenuity or concern to develop a workable way to provide income for a large segment of the population in poverty."[27] March's conclusion does not seem to be in conflict with Commissioner Ball's estimate that "perhaps a third to a half of the poverty that exists in the United States could be prevented by

---

[24]Robert M. Ball, "Is Poverty Necessary?" *Social Security Bulletin* (August 1965), p. 21.

[25]U.S., 86th Cong., 2d sess., *Report of the Advisory Council on Public Assistance* (January 1960), Sen. Doc. No. 93. For further information on which categories of the poor get public assistance see Morgan et al., *Income and Welfare in the United States,* Table 16–24.

[26]Michael S. March, "Poverty: How Much Will the War Cost?" *Social Service Review* 34 (June 1965), 149.

[27]Ibid.

the improvement and broader application of the social insurance principle."[28]

It is instructive to turn the question around and ask what would
happen to the poor if public transfers were sharply reduced. Would the
statistics show a sharp increase in the number of poor families, or would
there be more doubling up of families and more private transfers so that
the number of poor would be unchanged? Perhaps that is enough to
suggest that the benefits of transfers to the poor are not confined to those
we now count as poor.

---

[28]Ball, "Is Poverty Necessary?" p. 20. No estimate is offered of what this
would cost.

Chapter 7

PROJECTING RECENT POVERTY-REDUCTION TRENDS INTO THE FUTURE

WILL REDUCTION OF POVERTY BE SLOWER IN THE FUTURE?

It is argued by some that the future rate of poverty reduction will be slower because present-day poverty is qualitatively different from the poverty found in earlier days. Whereas old-time poverty was general, the new poverty, it is alleged, is specific and associated with a limited number of groups. These groups are in turn said to be those which are not likely to be helped by a generalized type of national economic growth because they are "immune" to such progress. This immunity allegedly arises out of personal characteristics or an environment which insulates them from opportunities for earning higher income.

John Kenneth Galbraith[1] wrote in 1958 of three kinds of poverty— generalized poverty, island poverty, and case poverty. The first is the kind which yields to the process of economic growth in which the average productivity of labor is increased. The latter two, he asserted, were the principal kinds of poverty then remaining in the United States and these are caused respectively by (1) inability or unwillingness to move out of low income areas or regions and (2)

> some quality peculiar to the individual or family involved— mental deficiency, bad health, inability to adapt to the discipline of modern economic life, excessive procreation, alcohol, insufficient education, or perhaps a combination of several of these handicaps. . . .[2]

Galbraith stated that, in the early 1950s, "The hard core of the very poor was declining, but not with great rapidity."[3] Further, he argued:

---

[1]*The Affluent Society* (Boston: Houghton Mifflin, 1958).
[2]Ibid., p. 325.
[3]Ibid., p. 324.

The most certain thing about modern poverty is that it is not efficiently remedied by a general and tolerably well-distributed advance in income. Case poverty is not remedied because the specific individual inadequacy precludes employment and participation in the general advance. Insular poverty is not directly alleviated because the advance does not necessarily remove the specific frustrations of environment to which the people of these islands are subject. This is not to say it has no effect. Secure job opportunities elsewhere, a concomitant of industrial advance, work against the homing instinct. And so, even more directly, does the spread of industrialization. The appearance of industry in parts of the Tennessee Valley area has had a strong remedial effect on the insular poverty of those areas. But it remains that advance cannot improve the position of those who, by virtue of self or environment, cannot participate or are not reached.[4]

We submit that Professor Galbraith has misinterpreted the low-income problem in several ways. In the first place, our finding that the percentage of the total population in low-income status fell from 26 in 1947 to 19 in 1957 and to 12 in 1967 would seem to contradict, or at least not to confirm, his statement that "the hard core of the very poor was declining but not with great rapidity." In the second place, with regard to island poverty, the record suggests that movement was a leading factor working for the reduction of numbers in low-income status. For instance, the number of rural farm families with income under $2000 (1947 dollars) actually fell during the 1947–57 period from 3.3 to 2.4 million because of movement off the farm (see Table 5.1). Similarly, there were great shifts among occupations and industries, which contributed to the reduction of low-income units. Next, with respect to "case poverty,"[5] it should be pointed out that some of these characteristics of persons are moderated over time. For example, average educational attainment levels rise simply because younger people at present have better education than older people. Hence, as the current generation of old people pass from the scene, the percentage of persons with low educational attainment falls.[6]

---

[4]Ibid., p. 327.

[5]Galbraith makes no reference to the important personal characteristics of age, color, and sex.

[6]Between 1950 and 1957 the median educational level increased one full year. "Most of the improvement was due to the fact that persons reaching adult ages . . . had been better educated than their parents and grandparents, many of whom were leaving the population through death" (U.S. Bureau of the Census, *Current Population Reports,* No. 77, p. 20). ". . . the educational level of young persons considerably exceeds that of older workers. In March 1957, 18- to 34-

The strong association of poverty with limited education may need to be underscored. While only 29 percent of all family heads have no more than eight grades of education, 60 percent of low-income heads are thus handicapped, and half of those with five or fewer years of schooling have low incomes (see Table 7.1).

The median level of educational attainment of the total population has been rising. The progress for young nonwhites has been especially rapid: nonwhites aged 20 to 24 had 9.2 years of schooling in 1950 as against 12.1 years for all those aged 20 to 24; by 1964 nonwhites had 12.1 years of schooling as compared to 12.5 for all those aged 20 to 24.[7]

Whether the reduction of poverty due to such improved levels of educational attainment should be attributed to economic growth or to social policy is a semantic problem. It is part of the adaptation to new and higher-skilled occupations and hard to separate from the whole process of growth. This process, in turn, pulls people into areas where educational opportunities are greater. This is not to deny that increased educational opportunity will not in itself contribute to the rate of growth. The changes in occupational status referred to above were no doubt facilitated by progress on the educational front.

Improved education is one of many factors that contributed to reduction of poverty within each broad group here examined.[8] Thus the incidence of poverty fell in each occupation, industry, and region. Poverty reduction was accomplished partly by intergroup movement and partly by intragroup improvement in average income levels. Additionally, some poverty reduction was achieved by an increasing flow of transfer payments to the poor.

Let us restate the question. Which groups among the contemporary low-income population are likely to diminish in the future, assuming a rising average level of income, and which ones are not likely to diminish? Do the answers to this question suggest a slowdown in the rate of poverty reduction?

---

year-old labor force members had completed over 12 years of school (on the average), as compared with only 9½ among middle aged workers and 8½ years among those over 65" (ibid., No. 78, p. 50).

[7]U.S., 88th Congr., 2d Sess., House of Representatives Committee on Education and Labor, *Poverty in the United States* (April 1964), p. 295.

[8]Terence F. Kelly, "Factors Affecting Poverty: A Gross Flow Analysis," *Technical Studies,* President's Commission on Income Maintenance Programs (Washington, D.C.: Government Printing Office, 1970), p. 35. Kelly estimates the elasticity of poverty with respect to education. He concludes that if all else stayed the same, but the number of family heads with less than an eighth-grade education were reduced by 1 percent, then the number of persons in poverty would decline by 0.14 percent.

Table 7.1. Percentage Distribution of All Families and of Low-Income Families, by Education of Head (1968)

| | Education of family head (grades) | | | | | | | |
	0–5	6–8	9–11	12	12 plus non-college training	Some college	College degree	Advanced degree	Total
All families	9%	20	17	17	12	11	10	4	=100%
Families with income under $3000	23%	35	19	8	6	6	2	1	=100%
Families in each educational class with income under $3000	50%	30	21	8	9	10	4	4	—

Source: 1968 Survey of Consumer Finances, Tables 1–5, 1–6.

WHAT GROUPS DO NOT BENEFIT BY ECONOMIC GROWTH?

It is true, of course, that some groups will not benefit from the process of growth in the same ways that others do. Those who are outside of the labor force tend to have an "immunity" to growth. (Here we are ignoring property income. Those who hold equity claims will tend to share in the growth of the economy thereby, even though they may be out of the labor force.) Those who cannot otherwise adapt to changes in the economic environment will run a greater risk of low-income status at some time in their lives than will others. In general, consumer-unit heads who are least mobile and adaptable are seen to have a handicapping characteristic such as old age, nonwhite color, female sex, or little education. Old age is a handicap in the sense that older people typically have greater difficulty in getting reemployed than do younger people and in getting into new and rapidly growing occupations and industries. (In one sense, the aged may be said to participate in growth if average Old Age Insurance and assistance payments rise with average income of the community. To the extent that the formula for computing Old Age, Survivors and Disability Insurance benefits accounts for rising average monthly wages, those benefits will rise over time.) Being nonwhite is a handicap to the extent that color may be a bar to higher-income occupations. Being female also operates to limit occupational choice and, to some extent, geographic mobility. Women with small children to care for have special income and expense problems. Families with only one parent are blocked from using a common escape route from poverty—sending a second adult into the labor force. Low educational attainment limits mobility and adaptability by barring entry to and perhaps limiting knowledge of and motivation toward new occupational possibilities.

It is significant that the contemporary low-income population is disproportionately made up of persons having one or more of these characteristics, as was seen above. It is estimated that while only 40 percent of the total population in 1967 had one or more of these three characteristics, 70 percent of the low-income population had one or more of them. It is plausible that each one of these characteristics has causal significance in determining the numbers in low-income status. As we have already mentioned, one can confidently predict that the numbers having low educational attainment will fall and from that deduce that the percent of persons having low income will fall. It also appears that the relative importance of the aged group of family heads will fall.

While low educational attainment and old age will diminish in importance over time, the other two "handicapping" characteristics of nonwhite color and being a female head of a household will not. The importance of families with female heads changed very little, but that of nonwhites increased from 8.3 to 10.0 percent between 1947 and 1967. Hence the next question is: Will economic growth reduce the incidence of low income among the aged, nonwhites, and female heads?

With regard to the aged, it is striking that 1947–57 saw virtually no improvement in their incomes. However, between 1957 and 1967 the percentage of aged with low incomes fell from 50 to 37. Therefore, on the basis of that experience we could identify this group as relatively "immune" to economic growth.

Female heads showed no improvement over the first postwar decade. In 1947, 47 percent of the families headed by women had incomes under $2000; in 1957, 49 percent had incomes that low. (This compares with percentages of 25 and 15 for all families.) In 1967, that percentage was down to 37. The failure of this rate to fall very much is doubtless due in part to the lower labor-force participation of female heads. The latter in turn is associated with the higher proportion of aged among women and also with the fact that many of the younger female heads have children to care for in the home. Hence, units with aged or female heads would seem to be identifiable as being "immune" to economic growth.

With respect to the third "handicapping" characteristic of nonwhite color, the picture is different. Nonwhite persons have shared and no doubt will continue to share in the processes of growth—i.e., higher earnings on present jobs, shifts into higher paying employments, and increasing numbers of earners per family. Between 1947 and 1957 and between 1957 and 1967 the percentage of nonwhite families with income under $2000 (1947 prices) fell from 61 to 45 to 28. The comparable percentages for white families were 25, 18, and 11. Hence, nonwhites are not immune to economic growth.

There are two other causal variables which should be accounted for in an appraisal of the "hard-core" nature of contemporary poverty. Some persons are disqualified from full participation in economic life because of physical or mental or emotional difficulties. Data are inadequate in this area, but some evidence is provided by a study of the prevalence of long-term disability. At the beginning of 1966 there were 17.8 million adults with a disability lasting more than six months.[9] More than 6 million of these persons were severely disabled—unable to work altogether or unable to work regularly—although they were under age 65. Of the latter

---

[9]Lawrence D. Haber, "Disability, Work, and Income Maintenance: Prevalence of Disability," *Social Security Bulletin* (May 1968), pp. 14–23. Of the 17.8 million long-term disabled, 12.5 million were not receiving any income maintenance benefits.

group, perhaps over half would have been in the labor force were they not disabled. How many of these disabled persons in fact had low incomes is not known. Nor is there any good way of estimating the importance of other related "personal" causes of low income, such as antisocial habits and attitudes or inability to adapt to the discipline of modern economic life. But we can say that disability does result in an important degree of immunity to economic growth.

Then there is the cause Galbraith refers to as "excessive procreation." While only one-fourth of the total population is found in families of six or over, one-third of low-income persons are in such large families. Looking to the future, it does not seem that very large families will increase as a proportion of all families, so this will not in itself cause an increasing share of all persons to be found in poverty. Further, large families are not immune to economic growth. In 1947–67 the incidence of low income fell at least as much for large families as it did for all families (see Table 4.1).

Table 7.2 summarizes this discussion. It underlines the conclusion that several factors are working against reduction, via economic growth, of the size of the low-income population. Four groups are identified as being highly immune to economic growth: those with little education, the aged, women, and the disabled. However, none of these groups will increase in relative importance in the total population in this decade. Yet, as progress against poverty goes on, these particular groups constitute a larger share of those who remain in poverty. The aged, the disabled, and female heads accounted for about one-third of the poverty group in 1957 and about one-half in 1967. It is this latter fact which makes it clear that economic growth alone will not bring about the elimination of poverty in the near future. Specialized income transfer programs will be necessary.

PROJECTING THE POVERTY RATE FOR 1977

Some of the factors that have worked to reduce poverty are not likely to continue. For example, the percentage rate of improvement in educational attainment will not be sustained; neither will the rate of movement off the farm. On the other hand, we foresee the arresting of a number of the demographic factors that have slowed poverty reduction in the recent past. Aged family heads will only increase by 9 percent between 1962 and 1975, while the total population will increase by 21 percent; families with three or more children will increase by only 14 percent, but the youngest family heads will increase by 132 percent. One result of the

Table 7.2. Importance of Selected Characteristics in Future Determination of Low-Income Population

Characteristic	Percent of low-income population with this characteristic 1967[a]	Will persons with this characteristic increase or decrease as percent of total population by 1977?	Degree to which persons with this characteristic are immune to economic growth
Low educational attainment of family head	56	Decrease	High
Old age	22	Decrease	High
Female head of family or unrelated individual	41	No change	High
Disability of nonaged family head	7	No change	High
Large family size (four or more children)	32	No change	Low
Nonwhite	31	Increase	Low

[a]See discussion of "Who Are the Poor," pp. 57–61, supra.

Table 7.3. Poor Persons and Families as Percent of Total Population, Selected Years (Forecasts in Parentheses)

	1947	1957	1959	1962	1967	1970	1975	1980
Percent of persons in poverty								
(Lampman)	26	19		18	12			
(Social Security Administration)			22	20	13			
Percent of families under $3000 (1962 or 1963 dollars)								
(Census)	32	23		20		(16)	(14)	
(Council of Economic Advisers)								(10–13)
(Gallaway)								(6–9)
(Gallaway corrected by Aaron)								(10–11)
(Madden)							(10)	

changing composition of the total population is that the composition of the poor is not likely to change radically by 1975.

Projecting the number of families that will be in poverty in the future is, of course, a hazardous undertaking. One projection made in 1964 by the Bureau of the Census assumed that the 1975 population would have the same incidence of poverty, i.e., income under $3000 in 1962 dollars, in each demographic group as in 1962, but also assumed that family incomes would rise by 2.5 percent per year. This yields an estimate that is slightly different for every demographic grouping, ranging from 7.7 to 8.6 million families but centering around 8 million, which would be 14 percent of all families. It also suggests that one-third or more of the aged, female heads, and nonwhites, and one-fourth of the southern families might still be poor in 1975.[10]

In retrospect, it appears that the 1964 projection was overly pessimistic. The projected percentage of families in poverty in 1975 was 14. Even if this is adjusted downward to 12 to bring it into line with other definitions of poverty, it is seen to be too high in the sense that the actual percentage of persons was already about that low in 1967 (see Table 7.3).

Another pessimistic projection, published in 1964 by W. H. Locke Anderson, was based on the frequency of incomes near to and far below the $3000 line in selected years.[11] A still more pessimistic projection was offered in that year by the Ad Hoc Committee on the Triple Revolution, who forecast steeply rising output per man-hour concurrent with increasing unemployment. Economic growth, they said, would not contribute to but would work against poverty reduction.

The rate of poverty reduction was much lower in 1956–62 than in the previous decade. This difference in rate prompted the Council of Economic Advisers to offer two estimates of 10 and 13 percent for 1980, one based on each of the earlier poverty-reduction rates. (Note that these are compatible with the Census projection cited above.) After an interesting exchange of views, Lowell E. Gallaway and Henry Aaron concluded in 1965 that a reasonable prediction was that 10–11 percent of families would have incomes under $3000 (1963 prices) in 1980.[12] This would imply that 8 to 9 percent of persons would be below

---

[10]*Poverty in the United States*, Table 23, p. 273.

[11]"Trickling Down: The Relationship between Economic Growth and the Extent of Poverty among American Families," *Quarterly Journal of Economics* 88 (November 1964), 511–24.

[12]For Gallaway's original paper see "The Foundations of the 'War on Poverty,'" *American Economic Review* 55 (March 1965), 122–30. Aaron's critique and Gallaway's reply are in ibid. 57 (December 1967), 1229–43.

the Census-SSA poverty lines in that year. As was mentioned earlier, the actual percentage below those lines was down to 13 in 1967, and hence well ahead of the schedule needed to reach the lower CEA projection of 10 percent for 1980. Writing somewhat later (1968), J. Patrick Madden concluded that the most favorable condition estimate would be 10 percent of families (8 percent of persons below SSA levels) not in 1980, but in 1975.[13] Madden's estimate looks like one toward which we were tracking in 1967. The poverty-income gap which is consistent with 8 percent of persons in poverty is about $5 billion. Of course, the actual outcome will depend on our experience with economic growth, the employment record of the poor, and the transfers received by the poor. But it appears unlikely that poverty will be completely eliminated in the United States before 1980 unless some new and extraordinary measures are taken.

---

[13]"Poverty Projections in Relation to Aggregate Demand, Economic Growth, and Unemployment," *Rural Poverty in the United States: A Report by the President's National Advisory Commission on Rural Poverty* (Washington, D.C.: U.S. Government Printing Office, 1968), 553–61.

PART C

Means To Accelerate the Process of Reducing Income Poverty

Chapter 8

A LISTING OF BROAD STRATEGIES

OPTIMISTIC VERSUS PESSIMISTIC OUTLOOK

Some writers have elected to portray the poverty problem in such a way as to convey a feeling of hopelessness. They refer to poor people as rejected, castoff, downtrodden, forgotten, and trapped in a vicious cycle of poverty breeding poverty. They allege that certain processes are cumulative, so that the poor are getting poorer, the immiseration of the proletariat is accelerating, and the poverty problem is swelling like some ugly cancerous growth. The method of characterization is a compound of Old Testament prophecy, Marxian economics, and gospel meeting eschatology. Poverty, it is said, is the work of national if not original sin; it will lead to, even if it will not be cured by, the downfall of capitalism or a religious or moral crisis. These writers assert that increasing deprivation indicates that existing remedies have all failed and that we need cataclysmic change in all social arrangements.

All this is best characterized as not very amusing nonsense. Poverty is not increasing. Reduction of income poverty and the filling of the poverty-income gap have been proceeding in recent years at the same time as, and partly because of, the fulfillment of other economic and social goals. The goal of poverty reduction rides a powerful following tide of economic growth and of successful social innovations. The sturdy framework of a tax-transfer system now stands available to accomplish greater redistribution of money, goods, and services. A determination to further reduce and finally to eliminate income poverty is consonant with a deep-running current in social science thought of recent decades.

Continuation of past policies and past experience for another decade may be expected to result in the virtual elimation of what may reasonably (by present standards) be thought of as "poverty"-income status. On the other hand, a relaxation in the rate of economic growth or a drop in the rate of increase of government transfer programs could make the goal of eliminating poverty recede into the far distant future. A higher rate of growth in average incomes, or a more aggressive government policy aimed at increasing the posttax, posttransfer share of total income received by the lowest fifth of consumer units (or a combination of both growth and wider sharing), could lead to this result in less than a decade.

Going beyond that general statement of conviction, we now ask: What are the specific policies which would most efficiently aid in promoting the speedy reduction of income poverty? As a first step in analyzing that question, we review the range of strategies suggested by the several lines of theory discussed in Parts A and B of this book; second, we discuss the considerations that enter into selecting among alternative strategies; and finally, we point to those strategies which seem to us most useful in the present situation. These have to do with employment and cash transfers.

It is necessary to restate a point made earlier about the goal under discussion. The poverty we are addressing is "income poverty," as distinct from a much broader definition of poverty which would encompass lack of such public services as education, lack of such privately supplied merit goods as health care and housing, lack of self-esteem, and lack of political participation or political power. Here we are considering the range of means against the criterion of what they would contribute to the reduction of income poverty. Some of the means which we pass by lightly may be justified as contributing to other types of antipoverty goals—or to even broader social goals—but we do not see them as having high priority in a short-run effort to abolish the remaining income poverty.

STRATEGY IMPLICIT IN THE PRESENT PROCESS

In Part B we reviewed the process by which poverty reduction takes place under the headings of (1) change in composition of population; (2) changes people make in search of higher incomes; and (3) change in income redistribution.

Changes in the composition of the population are not easily managed by social policy. Presumably immigration, family planning, and income maintenance policies all have a bearing on age composition, family size, and numbers of families headed by women. An immigration policy may be designed to exclude those who are likely to be poor or to compete with resident poor. Some family-planning studies are interpreted to show that low-income parents want the same number of children as do all others, but have substantially more. This suggests that making birth control information and methods, including legalized abortion and voluntary sterilization, more widely available would be an effective way to reduce poverty, Sar Levitan, among others, has urged this as the most cost-effective antipoverty measure. However, there are contrary interpretations of the data which claim that fertility differences are impossible to alter by educational efforts.

A similar controversy surrounds any income maintenance measure which would share the family's cost of having an extra child. For example, some critics allege that a family allowance will not reduce poverty because it will encourage poor parents to have more children. Others point to the antisocial nature of an Aid to Families with Dependent Children law which restricts payments for poor children to those whose fathers have abandoned them, and allege that this encourages such abandonment and thereby handicaps the child's chances of normal development. Presumably family composition could be influenced by a policy of paying benefits to intact families, and perhaps by imposing greater legal penalties on fathers who abandon their children.

Another part of the process of poverty reduction is indicated by changes people make in search of higher incomes. Our study shows that self-interest does work as a powerful engine to propel many people out of poverty. A strategy to accelerate poverty reduction might then include efforts to preserve and expand freedom and opportunities for individuals to move from low-income to high-income areas and occupations, and conversely for capital to flow toward the lower-income regions of the country. This strategy may well emphasize encouragement of more participation in economic progress by the nonwhites in the low-income population. Negroes, Indians, and other nonwhite minorities are often barred or alienated from such participation by occupational barriers and limited educational opportunities.

It has been noted that low-income status is particularly marked in rural areas, and more particularly in rural areas in certain regions of the country. Any program to overcome poverty must make special provision for this, offering rural people better opportunities to earn a satisfactory living. Such better opportunities may be brought about by (1) encouraging low-income farmers to move elsewhere, (2) encouraging nonagricultural employers to move their operations into these areas, and (3) offering technical and financial aid to improve the farming productivity of those who remain in agriculture. Ability and motivation of the next generation of adults in the depressed agricultural communities to achieve greater economic well-being would be improved by a sharply expanded program of education for those currently of school age.[1]

---

[1]See Report of the President's Commission on Rural Poverty, *The People Left Behind* (1968).

A third type of change which we discussed in Part B was change in income redistribution. It was concluded that progress in the elimination of poverty has been made with only a minor change in the share of income and wealth in the hands of the lowest fifth of consumer units. Faster progress might be made by more growth in transfer payments and more concentration on the share of those payments which go to the poor. Taxes can be redesigned to reduce the extraordinary burdens they now place upon the poor. In the longer run, greater transfers of educational, health, and other services to the poor will assist individuals to escape from poverty.

Groups within the low-income population vary in susceptibility to or immunity against the process of economic growth. In general, those groups with low labor-force participation are quite immune—the aged, the disabled, and the family units headed by women. The long-run private approaches to reducing the incidence of poverty within these groups are many, including more saving, more private insurance, improved family responsibility, and adaptation of employment opportunities to the needs and limitations of aged persons and women with family responsibilities. Public approaches, on the other hand, include the provision of more funds for social insurance and public assistance programs. These programs in turn can be associated with guidance, counseling, retraining and re-habilitation work aimed at increasing participation in the economic life of the community.

Income redistribution can be changed to meet needs of the poor not only by expansion of existing transfer payments, but also by innovations which would extend income supplementation to those given least favorable treatment by the present system of cash transfers, namely the "working poor" and children.

To continue our survey of the possible strategies against poverty, we next turn to those strategies which flow out of various explanations of why people are poor.

STRATEGIES BASED ON THEORIES OF SELECTION FOR POVERTY

The three theories about causes of poverty reviewed in chapter 2 at pages 36–37 show ways in which our system selects people to be poor. These have to do with risks, barriers, and personal differences. Some remedies are suggested by this three-point analysis.

It is consonant with the "risk" theory that poverty will be minimized to the extent that frequency of disability, premature death, family breakup, loss of savings, and unemployment can be reduced. To the extent that a basic risk cannot be done away with, individuals, private groups, and governments can take steps to insure against the loss of income associated with the risk.

Poverty is sometimes seen as the result of failure of successive lines of defense against it. The first line of defense is earnings. The second line of defense is property income and savings. The third line is insurance, assistance, and charity. Note that this phrasing of the problem seems to assume that the normal position is nonpoverty and that the problem is to prevent people from falling away from this norm. However, some may never have reached the norm in the first place. Another framework for consideration of risk is suggested by what might be called the life-cycle classification of causes of poverty according to phase of life. Some persons are born into poverty. Others enter it in childhood because of death or disability of a parent. Some enter it in adulthood because of a personal disaster or failure to insure against all risks. In this "risk theory" the emphasis is upon randomness and historical accident, as in a fable Carl Sandburg told of two cockroaches washed off a roof by a rainstorm. One fell in a rock pile and the other in a garbage pail. When they met again the first cockroach asked the other, "How does it happen that you are so fat while I am so lean?" The answer was, "It is because of my foresight, industry and thrift."

A second class of remedies, which are identified with the "social barriers" theory of poverty, includes such things as breaking down practices of racial discrimination in hiring, housing, and education; improving mobility of labor from rural to urban occupations; and bettering chances for women and elderly people to work in a wider range of occupations. These remedies also include improving the environment of the poor and integrating the poor with the rest of the community. William Penn alternated the wide and narrow streets in Philadelphia so that the rich and poor would know each other.

The "social barriers" theory says that if poor people are different from the nonpoor, it is because of the fact of poverty rather than because of innate traits. One hundred years ago the Irish drank because they were poor, rather than vice versa. According to this theory, poverty itself is what is transmitted. It is an inheritable disease. The observable personal differences which are asserted to be symptoms rather than causes will abate if the conditions of poverty are remedied. Here the analogy to public health matters is clear.

A third theory is that people are selected to be poor on the basis of personal differences (which may or may not be transmissible) of ability, of motivation, of moral character, of will and purpose. Some philosophers consider life a matter of survival of the fittest and a contest which rewards the morally as well as the financially elect, and appropriately visits the punishments and rewards unto the second or third generation. However, if we want to reduce poverty, we may strive to reduce personal differences of ability and motivation. Here again there is a wide range of steps that can be taken—including steps to improve the health of the poor. The statistics on mental retardation at birth show a strong income effect and a relationship with lack of prenatal care. We currently spend over $50 billion on health care; $8 billion of that is spent through public channels, and the rest of it is spent privately. Probably the lowest fifth of families, ranked by income, receive health goods and services which are valued at less than one-fifth of all such services.

We currently spend over $36 billion on public and private education in this country. This expenditure undoubtedly has much to do with our success in reducing poverty, and further increases in educational outlay per person may make contributions toward that end. Many researchers who believe that performance in school is heavily conditioned by pre-school experience, urge that formal school experience should start as early as age two. Quite apart from overall considerations, it is possible to slant increases of educational outlay more toward the poor. While the lowest fifth of the families, ranked by income, have one-fifth of the children, it is safe to estimate that less than one-fifth of the total educational outlay is spent on their behalf. Morgan and his colleagues found that children in the lowest income families go to schools where the expenditure per child is 13 percent below the national average. Only 45 percent of the children of the poor complete high school, in contrast to a national average of 65 percent.[2]

STRATEGIES EMPLOYED SINCE COLONIAL TIMES

In chapter 1 we discussed four strategies against poverty which have been employed in this country since its colonial beginnings. These are (1) to establish and facilitate the working of a market system aimed at economic growth and maintenance of high employment; (2) to adapt the system to the needs of the poor; (3) to change the poor and adapt them to the system; and (4) to relieve the distress of the poor. In the following discussion we will collapse number (4) into (2).

---

[2]James Morgan, David Martin, Wilbur J. Cohen, and Harvey Brazer, *Income and Welfare in the United States* (New York: McGraw-Hill, 1962).

Make the Existing System Work Better

We have asserted that free market forces and ordinary self-interest operate within a well-functioning economy to achieve more exits from than retreats into poverty from year to year. It would seem to follow that there should be an emphasis upon aggregative measures of fiscal and monetary policy and general market measures aimed at encouraging efficiency of production.

We concluded in chapter 7 that any downgrading of the importance of high employment and rapid economic growth both in preventing massive increases in the numbers of poor and in reducing poverty is misguided. Over half the poor family heads are in the labor force, and 70 percent of poor families have at least one earner. This degree of association of poverty and wage-earning is heightened if we consider number of *persons* rather than *families* in poverty. It is true that the nonlabor-force heads have increased as a percentage of all poor-family heads since 1947, but the demographic trends which are partly responsible for this are not expected to continue. Indeed, the reverse is true, with the greatest swelling of the adult population expected from the younger age groups.

Not only is poverty closely associated with labor-force participation on a cross-sectional basis, but the rate of poverty reduction appears to be responsive to the rate of economic growth. The largest yearly reductions in the number of families in poverty occur in those years when average incomes increase the most, although it is possible to interpret the data as indicating a slight decline in the degree of responsiveness over time. Lowell Gallaway disputes even the latter point. He concludes, therefore, that there is relatively little case for "substantial anti-poverty programs of a selective character. . . . Rather, greater consideration should be given to the role which economic growth can play in eliminating poverty."[3] Gallaway apparently believes that seeking to reduce unemployment below 4 percent or to further improve the rate of growth would be efficient ways to achieve a faster rate of poverty reduction. However, few would argue that any employment and growth combination that is feasible would, by itself, eliminate poverty in the near future.

The argument about the structural nature of contemporary poverty has an aridity to it that is reminiscent of the controversy concerning the allegedly rising significance of structural unemployment after 1957. It poses a hard choice only if the needs for growth dictate that there should

---

[3] "The Foundations of the 'War on Poverty,'" *American Economic Review* 55 (March 1965), 122–31.

be no "substantial anti-poverty programs of a selective character," or vice versa. It should be possible to pursue both lines of policy simultaneously, and it may be that the two lines can reinforce one another. For example, if the growth of aggregate demand requires expenditure for public works, they could be concentrated in areas where poverty incidence is high; if a tax cut is called for, it could be slanted toward the poor rather than the rich. If investment in education and training and relocation are seen as ways to increase the nation's economic capacity, those investments can be aimed at the poor. The benefits of growth policy could be made to trickle up rather than down. This kind of slanting may not be the most efficient route to growth, but it need not be that such special antipoverty efforts are antithetical to a satisfactory rate of growth. Beyond this, it may be possible to accelerate the rate of poverty reduction by adapting the system to confront certain causes of poverty.

Adapt the System to the Needs of the Poor

While some see the "slow" reduction of poverty amid rising affluence as a consequence of failure of the existing system to operate properly, others see it resulting from failure to modify the system sufficiently to reach the needs of the poor. If it is viewed as the latter, it could be interpreted as ironic, since many adaptations (e.g., Social Security, collective bargaining, farm and housing subsidies, and progressive taxation) have already been made under antipoverty banners. As Irving Kristol observes (perhaps incorrectly), "Poverty, after all, was the problem the welfare state most particularly set out to solve."[4]

Some have argued that if we simply modify the rationale and extend the application of existing policies to the remainder of the poor, then a substantial part of the poverty problem can be cut away without waiting for 1980. The adaptations that can be made under this general heading include dealing more directly with specific locations, conditions, and problems encountered by the poor; developing the economies of areas that can be identified as pockets of poverty; legislating and bargaining low wage rates up to above-poverty levels; offering training and retraining to qualify low-income workers for higher-skill jobs; providing jobs for all able-bodied poor by subsidizing private employers (including self-employed farmers) and by public work or work relief; prohibiting discriminatory barriers to employment on account of color, age, sex, or education; expanding and supplementing presently operating transfer payment programs to block more completely retreats into poverty and to narrow the poverty-income gap.

---

[4] "The Poverty of Equality," *The New Leader* (March 1, 1965), pp. 15–16.

A quite different way to order the discussion of ways to adapt the system to the needs of the poor is to review, following the marginal principle, the seven stages of transfer set out in chapter 6. Do we want more or less transferring to take place via each of the following? (1) Subsidy to raise certain factor incomes (work relief or wage subsidy to workers or private employers); (2) employer coverage of risk for employees; (3) tax-financed cash and in-kind transfers; (4) nonemployer-financed private insurance; (5) subsidy to lower the market price of a consumer good; (6) transfers by philanthropic organizations; and (7) interfamily transfers.

At this point in time, controversy ranges over the several stages and the several tax and transfer redistributive patterns. There are live proposals that government serve as employer of last resort and that government subsidize on-the-job training (stage 1); that public education, health, and housing benefits be slanted more clearly toward the poor (stage 3); that voluntary health insurance, compulsory health insurance, and public provision of health care be brought into new balance; and that rent subsidies and food subsidies be expanded (stage 5). Additionally, there are proposals that our existing programs of cash transfers should be reformed, or that new types of cash benefits should be introduced (stage 3).

Choices will need to be made among the possible increases in transfers. In making these choices, the redistributive pattern may be significantly altered. However, it is clear that the system could, if we were willing to pay the price, be so adapted to the needs of the poor that, assuming no great reversal of the overall workings of the system, poverty could be reduced at a rate well above that of recent years. It is interesting to speculate about why we have not done more in adapting the system to the needs of the poor. (Some find it equally interesting to speculate about why we have done as much as we have in this direction.) Is it a fear and mistrust of the poor by the nonpoor majority, or is it more the result of the inability of the poor minority to mount effective protest? Is it, as Nathan Glazer suggests, the result of excessive emphasis upon individualism and localism in the face of racial and ethnic diversity?[5] Have we bogged down in what Richard Titmuss called "the troubled area between equality and the needs of the poor for unequal treatment"? Are we hung forever on the present balance among principles in the income maintenance field and unwilling to relent somewhat in the emphasis upon assuring continuity of income, via the insurance principle of equity,

---

[5]"Sociologist's View of Poverty," in Margaret Gordon, ed., *Poverty in America* (San Francisco: Chandler Publishing Co., 1965), pp. 12–26.

as opposed to assuring adequacy of income? Have we run out of imagination concerning ways to extend the positive sanctions for dependency
we now have to new categories, say to children in poor but otherwise
normal homes? Or is the reason why we have not done more to adapt the
system founded on the belief that all such plans are foredoomed unless,
as a prior condition, the poor themselves are changed?

Changing the Poor to Fit the System

According to a third theory, the basic cause of poverty is the culture,
informal social organization, and personal socialization of deprived individuals. Hence the remedies for poverty are to be found in therapy on
a case-by-case basis, especially adapted education, radical change in the
social environment, and small-group, self-help organizations of the poor.
According to this theory, the goals, attitudes, and motivations of the poor
and the subculture that carries the values alien to the nonpoor culture
must be fundamentally changed. The intergenerational cycle of poverty
breeding poverty must be broken before the escape from poverty that
a well-functioning economy offers can be meaningful.

Students of poverty have long noted that the poor are different,
alien, even barbarous (as George Bernard Shaw called them), and few
have argued that poverty is character building. But there has always been
debate over the question put by Sir Benjamin Thompson in 1790: "To
make vicious and abandoned people happy, it has generally been sup-
posed necessary to make them virtuous. But why not reverse this order?
Why not make them first happy, and then virtuous?" Many have concluded with Jeremy Bentham that "the conduct of the poor will depend—
not upon the remote and casual influence of the rich, but upon the direct
and constant exercise of plastic power."[6] Sidney and Beatrice Webb
included, along with prevention, universal provision, and curative treatment, the principle of compulsion among their remedies for poverty.

Some who depart from a cultural view of poverty conclude that the
object is to exclude the poor (reduce immigration and discourage internal
migration and integration) and seek to reduce their reproduction (promote
sterilization and birth control among the poor, avoid a family allowance
or any other incentives to larger family sizes among the poor). Others
are more optimistic concerning the possibility of transforming the poor;
they remain unimpressed by assertions that poor children are notably

---

[6]*The Works of Jeremy Bentham* (Edinburgh: London, Simpkin, Marshall
& Co., 1843), p. 395.

inferior in genetic terms and pin their hopes on environmental improvement, the transmission of general community values to children, and ultimately on the appeal of opportunities to join the nonpoor majority. They put their emphasis upon breaking down the cultural isolation of the poor by roads, schools, mass media, city planning to intermix poor and nonpoor neighborhoods, and upon special efforts to reduce infant mortality and birth defects.

Specific remedies in this category include rehabilitative work with physically handicapped and disturbed persons, family counseling and consumer education, urban redevelopment, area development with emphasis on community facilities, special health services that reach out for, rather than merely wait for, cases of medical need, preschool and extraschool experiences to widen the horizons of culturally deprived youngsters. A method much favored by those who espouse the third theory is the development of local, indigenous leadership and community organization which can make effective use of outside technical assistance.

Many of these remedies are in effect now and the question is how far and how fast to extend them. Some critics have claimed that most of the contemporary American poor are not isolated and alienated and would respond favorably to better job opportunities or to more transfer payments. I suppose all are agreed that most of the "change the poor" remedies would be more effective if the poor were not so poor and if they had clearer evidence that self-reform would lead to better employment prospects. But also, all are agreed that some programs to change the attitudes, motivations, and potential productivity of the poor—and particularly of poor children—can make an independent contribution to a faster rate of poverty reduction, allowing for a time lag of one or two decades. There are outstanding examples of success with programs of this kind, and there assuredly are cases of poverty which appear to be beyond the reach of broad-based economic reform of the types discussed earlier.

Chapter 9

CONSIDERATIONS IN SELECTING
ALTERNATIVE MEANS

Chapter 8 reviews the possible methods to use in an antipoverty campaign with reference to the process of poverty reduction and to broad theories of causation. That review casts up a range of testable predictive propositions. They are of the form that if we do this, income poverty will be reduced, or the poverty-income gap will be narrowed.[1] The policy variables touched upon include monetary-fiscal policies, area redevelopment, minimum wage laws, transfers (both in cash and noncash forms) and tax revision, public work, immigration and population policies, plans to minimize isolation and concentration of the poor, rehabilitation and special health and education and training efforts, and self-help organizations of the poor.

RELATIONSHIPS AMONG ENDS AND MEANS

How do we then select from this range the methods to use? How do we decide that certain methods are unacceptable or that some are to be preferred? These questions involve matters for judgment akin to the setting of the goal. Among them are decisions about whether one wants to encourage a few major programs versus a large number of special programs, whether to favor general measures versus those that are specific to the poor (some of the remedies involve paying out more benefits to the non-poor than to the poor), whether one wants to deal broadside with all the poor or selectively with certain groups among the poor, perhaps singling out those in the most "grinding" poverty, or those who are not only poor but have some other handicap as well and have the least basis for

---

[1]The succeeding type of proposition is: if we reduce income poverty, then certain consequences will follow. Consequential propositions of this sort are discussed in chapter 2.

hope. Some might prefer to emphasize aid to those who simultaneously have low incomes and lack access to public facilities.

Some might reject a method because it does or does not involve a high degree of centralization or coordination, or because it leaves out participation in planning and execution by private parties including the affected poor, or because it involves a high degree of compulsion or a heavy tax burden for some. In the political process there may be certain values which will play a significant role in selecting from the array of testable propositions for experiment. Some proposals will have great appeal because they appear to relate closely to values other than income adequacy, e.g., self-reliance, family solidarity, fair prices or wages, local autonomy or states' rights, voluntarism, or community spirit and fellowship.

What goals or values are we willing to compromise for a gain in the speed of poverty reduction? Should we depart from our traditional emphasis upon self-reliance and individual initiative to recognize positive sanctions for new patterns of dependency along the lines suggested by schemes for a guaranteed minimum income for all? Should we override states' rights and local autonomy in pursuit of a national minimum of benefits and services to the poor? Should we, in other words, downgrade certain "process goals" to make way for the "performance goal" of reducing poverty?

Perhaps that is enough to indicate that, by setting out an antipoverty goal, President Johnson did more than restate traditional purposes. His declaration carried with it a whole set of potentially disturbing questions about prevailing goals and attitudes. It challenged us to ask whether there are policies and practices in effect which, while originally justified as a means to an end, may now be perpetuated as ends in themselves.

But this confusion of ends and means is a near and present danger in the statement of the antipoverty goal itself. Antipoverty work should be distinguished from a generalized helping and doing good for people. Many people have trouble distinguishing the income-poverty problem from other problems such as unequal protection of the laws, lack of education, lack of housing, lack of health services, delinquency and crime, limited citizen participation, spiritual and cultural deprivation, lack of fellowship, and geographic isolation. These problems are not exclusive to the poor; if government sets out to help the sick and disturbed, or those who need or want better housing, not only may the greater part of the help go to the nonpoor but it may do precious little to reduce income poverty.

In instituting antipoverty programs there is danger that these programs will be identified as "good things," that we may never get around to measuring whether the original end is being accomplished and, if so, whether the programs have had anything to do with it. The confusion is only somewhat lessened if we insist that the programs be of benefit to the poor exclusively. Poverty reduction does not mean merely "doing something for the poor" any more than economic growth means "doing something for business." There is value in continually relating means back to the end.

It is important to note how different this goal-oriented thinking is from the theories of "government by pressure group" that picture government as a service agency whose function it is to respond to the felt needs of its constituents. According to these theories, government does not pursue national goals but seeks a workable balance among the wishes of private interests, all of which are seeking government support. Some would even go so far as to argue that statements of national economic goals are merely slogans rationalizing a particular pattern of distribution of government largesse. Hence they would urge that it is inequitable to insist upon a higher standard of goal achievement where the poor are involved than where other groups are involved.

FOUR CONFLICTING MENTALITIES

It may help us appreciate the complex relationships among ends and means to identify four "mentalities" or approaches or emphases which are advanced in discussions of taxation and expenditures for health, education, and welfare. These may be called the *minimum-provision* mentality, the *replacement of loss* mentality, the *horizontal and vertical equity* mentality, and the *efficiency of investment* mentality. The first mentality is the one which has traditionally guided public assistance, public housing, and health care and other special services for the poor. Here the emphasis is upon the adequacy of the benefit for those who are unable to provide any part of the necessary item. Little attention is paid to the equities vis-à-vis those who are able to pay part of the cost of a minimum provision. The purpose is essentially defensive and crisis oriented.

The "replacement of loss" mentality finds expression in insurance, both private and social. Here the emphasis is on the sharing of loss without reference to need, but with attention to the several parties' ability to pay and ability to prevent the loss. This mentality traditionally has little concern for the need identified by public assistance, but concentrates on irregularities of income, or expenditure (as for health), experienced by regular members of the labor force.

The "horizontal and vertical equity" mentality is most fully developed in the individual income tax. The emphasis is on treating equally all those who are similarly stationed and narrowing inequality among the groups ranked in a superior to inferior relationship. This mentality comes into direct conflict with the two previously discussed mentalities when it is proposed that a negative income tax should replace some or all public assistance and social insurance benefits. The advocate of the negative income tax tends to view with horror the categorical exclusions, the abrupt withdrawal of benefits, the high marginal tax rates, and the capricious changes of rank order of families in both public assistance and social insurance. On the other hand, advocates of the latter charge that the income tax mentality has no motive power to expand, since its goal of narrowing inequality is vague and formless and, to some, alarming. The controversy among persons of competing mentalities is often exacerbated by mutual misunderstanding of vocabularies as well as concepts and practices which are peculiar to each.

The fourth mentality is that of "efficiency of investment," wherein the goal is not equity but improvement of the quantity or quality of final output. The recipient of the transfer or distributive allocation (e.g., a higher education subsidy) is seen as a means to an end (e.g., a higher national product in some future year). The issue is not equity in the distribution of the benefits. Neither is it assuring a minimum provision. Rather, it is to reach a favorable relationship between the costs to the society and the benefits which will flow from those costs.

These four mentalities are presently expressed in our system of transfers. None of them speaks to the strong points of any of the others, yet each puts some constraint on the others. Perhaps what we see evolving in this late stage of growth of the national system of transfers is a new balance—or tension—among the four mentalities.

RELATIVE EFFECTIVENESS OF PROGRAMS IN REDUCING POVERTY

All the above political and philosophical constraints and more may enter into the framework within which antipoverty programs are to be judged. But a key step in the decisionmaking process should be a judgment concerning the relative effectiveness of the several possible programs in reducing income poverty and in filling the poverty-income gap.

In calculating the result, some weighting might be given for the shortness of time required, for the success with hard cases, for the distance people are moved past the poverty line, and for additions to the incomes of the nonpoor. The results should be related to the costs, and these, too, must be calculated in more than one form, with weights assigned to the different forms. There are programs where all the costs are tax costs, and there are others where the primary burden is not in the form of taxes but of extra effort or higher prices paid by private parties (including, in some cases, the poor). The cost of some programs will include disincentive effects which are measurable in terms of lost national product. When all the benefits and costs are known, one can calculate a cost-benefit ratio, and when this is done for two or more programs, including the status quo, one has a basis for choosing one program over another. Logically, one could include the preferences concerning methods and groups to be served in the cost-benefit formulations. Table 9.1 shows a form for relating the concepts of benefit-cost analysis to any particular antipoverty program.

Table 9.1.   Form for Estimating Benefit-Cost Ratios for Any Particular Antipoverty Program

	Poor population	Nonpoor population	Total population
Benefit (plus or minus)			
Added income			
wages			
transfers			
Less forgone income			
wages			
transfers			
Added potential for future wage income			
Weighted total benefit			
Cost (plus or minus)			
Added taxes			
Addition to prices paid			
Loss of leisure			
Weighted total cost			
Benefit-cost ratio (weighted total benefit divided by weighted total cost)			

Yearly change in number of poor persons per unit of weighted total cost =_____.
Yearly change in size of poverty-income gap per unit of weighted total cost =____.

However, even the narrowly conceived cost-benefit ratios for competing antipoverty methods require facts and information about functional relationships which we do not now have. In many cases the causal link-ages from original input to result are intricate. Suppose, for example, that funds are appropriated for preschool training. How much does this affect a child's performance in high school and how much does this improve his chance of escaping from poverty? Suppose in the meantime his parents receive a family allowance and he is given a part-time job in the Neighborhood Youth Corps. Does each program reinforce the other? If so, by how much?

Other examples will indicate why it is uncertain what the effects of some of these adaptations may be, on balance, in reducing poverty. Thus it is not clear that taxing growing areas of the economy to make more capital available to declining regions is going to contribute more to poverty reduction in the latter than it subtracts from poverty reduction in the former, or that mobility of capital into a depressed area is less wasteful than mobility of labor out of the area to more prosperous areas. (We should note, however, that the development of community facilities such as roads and schools, by reducing cultural isolation, may actually encourage out-migration.)

Similarly, it is not clear that legislating a higher minimum wage does more for those who keep their jobs at the higher rate than it disadvantages those who may be dismissed or may not find jobs because of the higher minimum. There can be no disputing that many of the poor are in rela-tively poor regions (almost half the poor are in the South) and many people earn low wages (at least 10 million workers got less than $1.50 per hour in 1967), and it is clear that development of those regions and legislating away those low wage rates would help some of those who are poor. But this may be one of those cases in economics in which around the barn is the shortest way home. The unintended side effects may or may not more than offset the direct positive effects. Such side effects arise in connection with many policies. For another example, consider this hypothetical case: if agricultural price policy were to raise the price of all food by 10 percent, this would amount to a 3 percent tax on the incomes of many poor families, thus helping some farmers, many of whom are not poor, at the expense of all other families, some of whom are poor.

The judgments become all the more complicated as we admit the possibility that choices on the redistribution front may have effects on the aggregative front. As Eveline Burns stated, "The willingness to sacri-fice the maximum of economic output in order to insure a distribution of income that commends itself to the majority as being more acceptable and socially stable can be condemned as irrational or as unwise only if it is made without adequate knowledge of the degree of sacrifice of output accompanying the selected redistributive measures."[2] A few notes on possible losses and gains may be in order. Availability of cash transfers, which often have both "income" and "substitution" effects, may induce workers to retire earlier and take more leisure; increased taxation may cause less saving and hence less capital formation; payroll taxes may lead employers to substitute capital for labor; higher labor costs may make American products less competitive in export markets. On the other hand, the automatic stabilizing effect of Social Security expenditures and taxes may make the economy more resistant to recessionary and inflationary tendencies; education and health outlays may make contributions to improved productivity; raising living standards of the poor may allow for reduction of some community costs and reduction of taxes on the nonpoor; social insurance may induce employers to prevent accidents and regularize employment. Some of these measures may modify the primary distribution of income and the pattern of family formation.

All these questions about the costs and benefits of antipoverty measures are, in principle, answerable, but the fact is we don't know how to answer them now even though some of these questions are as old as economics. The sad situation is that we have not been measuring the effectiveness of many "grand experiments" in public policy. In the postwar years we have increased per capita social welfare expenditures by 336 percent, in constant dollars (see Table 6.2). Yet there have been few studies of the effect these expenditures have had on the rate of poverty reduction. This poverty of empirical research is not unique to the problem here under consideration. George J. Stigler made lack of testing the effectiveness of many basic policies (including some antipoverty polices) the subject of his presidential address at the 1964 meetings of the American Economic Association.[3] Hence, progress that is being made in developing cost-benefit ratios for alternative antipoverty programs has significance not only for the war on poverty but for all social science in its application to public policy.[4]

---

[2]*Social Security and Public Policy* (New York: McGraw-Hill, 1956), p. 276.

[3]"The Economist and the State," *American Economic Review* 55 (March 1965), pp. 1–18. Also see Daniel P. Moynihan, "The Professors and the Poor," *Commentary* 46 (August 1968), 19–28.

[4]Examples of studies that pursue this program are: Glen Cain, "Benefit-Cost Estimates for the Job Corps" (Discussion Paper No. 9, Institute for Research on Poverty, University of Wisconsin, 1967); and Thomas I. Ribich, *Education and Poverty* (Washington, D.C.: Brookings Institution, 1968). A pathbreaking use of experimental techniques to measure costs and benefits of variations of negative income taxation is currently being made in the so-called

But in the meantime decisions have to be made about ways to speed the rate of poverty reduction. The lack of complete information should not necessarily inhibit decisionmakers more in this field than it does in others. Neither should it be allowed to cancel out the use of the best estimates of costs and benefits that can be made.[5] The best way to achieve a purpose is to state clearly what the goal is, to list all the possible means to the goal, to select and implement those means which have the greatest benefits (or advantages) net of costs (or disadvantages), keeping in mind that experience, research and reflection, objective conditions, and democratic processes can lead to changes in the nature of the goal, the list of possible means, and the estimate of benefits and costs associated with the several means.[6]

Those who are making policy for the war on poverty, no less than policy-makers in other fields, find that all these elements are gloriously entangled. They calculate benefits and costs with reference to numerous values or goals of various sorts. Their decision of how fast and how far to go with how many means involves a decision about the priority among all national goals of the antipoverty goal. Only if the latter were the only goal would it follow that every means that promised to contribute anything to that goal should be employed to the fullest.

DISCUSSION OF SOME SELECTED MEANS

It is with the foregoing broad considerations in mind that we turn now to a discussion of three of the most widely favored means for accelerating

---

New Jersey experiment with 1000 families over a three-year period. The experiment is described by Harold W. Watts in "Graduated Work Incentives: An Experiment in Negative Taxation," *American Economic Review* 59 (May 1969), 463–72 (Reprint No. 39, Institute for Research on Poverty, University of Wisconsin, 1969).

[5] For a valuable discussion of the usefulness and difficulties of cost-benefit study, see Alice M. Rivlin, "The Planning, Programming, and Budgeting System in the Department of Health, Education, and Welfare: Some Lessons from Experience" (Reprint No. 162, Washington, D.C.: Brookings Institution, 1969). Also see Dr. Rivlin's forthcoming Gaither lectures, *Systematic Thinking and Social Action,* wherein she makes the point that programs should be designed to yield information about their effectiveness.

[6] The tentative nature of the first steps in the war on poverty was emphasized by President Johnson in his 16 March 1964 message to Congress. He said, "It [the Economic Opportunity Act] will also give us a chance to test our weapons, to try our energy and ideas and imagination for the many battles yet to come. As conditions change, and as experience illuminates our difficulties, we will be prepared to modify our strategy."

the process of poverty reduction.[7] These are (1) jobs, (2) cash transfers, and (3) services for the poor.

1. More and Better Jobs for the Poor

The historical process of poverty reduction depends upon improvement of labor productivity. For this to occur at a steady rate there must be continuing improvement in technology, organization, and management; increasing quantities of capital per worker; and willingness of workers to adapt to new techniques in new industries and new localities. There must also be a steady improvement in the average quality of labor. The *potential* to produce is distinguishable from the *actual* or realized level of production, which tends to vary considerably more than the potential. A rough index of the degree to which actual product differs from the potential is the percent of the labor force that is unemployed. If we can maintain a constant level of unemployment while improving potential to produce at 3 percent per man per year, poverty reduction can proceed at a fair rate. But, if we can simultaneously cut down the level of unemployment, poverty reduction can go faster. The high rate of poverty reduction from 1964 to 1969 was in part due to the reduction in unemployment from 5.5 percent to 3.5 percent. It appears that a one-point reduction in unemployment brings a reduction in poverty of about 1.5 million persons. (It also yields an increase in national product of over $30 billion.) The poor benefit from lower unemployment in several ways. First, some of the unemployed members of poor families get jobs. Second, some of those employed work longer hours and hence have higher weekly wages. Third, some members of poor families who have not been counted as unemployed because they were not actively seeking work are encouraged to seek and find jobs. This "encouraged worker" phenomenon means that some families rise out of poverty because of the earnings of secondary workers. Fourth, high employment means that employers have to reach farther down into the ranks of relatively unqualified workers and adapt jobs to them and train them. This helps to qualify them for

---

[7] I have been influenced by the following valuable studies on this topic. James Tobin, "Raising the Incomes of the Poor," in Kermit Gordon, ed., *Agenda for the Nation* (Washington, D.C.: Brookings Institution, 1968), pp. 77–116; James L. Sundquist, "Jobs, Training, and Welfare for the Underclass," in ibid., pp. 49–76; Joseph A. Kershaw, *Government against Poverty* (Washington, D.C.: Brookings Institution, 1970); Robert A. Levine, *The Poor Ye Need Not Have with You: Lessons from the War on Poverty* (Cambridge, Mass.: M.I.T. Press, 1970).

future advancement. Fifth, the poor benefit from high employment because it appears that wages for low-skill work rise more than other wages in such situations.

These five factors were much in evidence in the years 1964–69. However, it would have been hard for them to work at the same pace in the years immediately after that. To do so, we would have had to take unemployment down from 3.5 to 1.5 percent of the labor force. The lowest unemployment rate recorded in this country was 2 percent in one year in World War II. The 3.5 percent unemployment rate of 1969 was induced by the expansionary fiscal policy started by the discretionary tax cut of 1964 and continued by the deficit financing of part of the $30 billion increase of defense expenditures for Vietnam beginning in 1965. Unemployment was drawn down in part by the build-up of the Armed Forces by 700,000 men and the increase in civilian employment in defense industries by about 1 million workers. As total demand and total employment rose, employers found that they could increase output only by bidding employees away from each other and by hiring less efficient workers out of the unemployed pool. In any event, wages and costs of production went up and prices went up. In 1968 prices rose 4.7 percent and in 1969, 6 percent. These are much higher rates of inflation than we had had in earlier years and threatened to cause us trouble with the balance of payments. From the point of view of short-run poverty reduction, it might have been desirable to keep tightening the labor market still further.[8] But more general considerations militated against blithe expansionism.

According to one theory, the thing that causes inflation to appear whenever unemployment is lower than 4 percent is the speed with which unemployment has been drawn down. This "speed limits" theory says that we should expect inflation to abate if unemployment stays below 4 percent for some time and is only gradually reduced a few tenths of a point at a time. According to this theory, the cure for inflation is to increase productivity by forcing employers to adapt to a permanently tight labor market and encouraging nonparticipants to come into the labor force and to make costly moves and training efforts. To the extent that workers can be retrained to fit vacant jobs and informed of such vacancies

---

[8]The gain by the poor in terms of extra earnings tends to exceed their loss in purchasing power from assets bearing a fixed yield. Social insurance benefits tend to keep up with inflation. Moreover, the burden of long-term debt is eased by inflation. For a review of the facts on this see Robinson G. Hollister and John L. Palmer, "The Impact of Inflation on the Poor" (Discussion Paper No. 40, Institute for Research on Poverty, University of Wisconsin, 1969).

by an "active labor market policy" of the Swedish type, the inflationary consequences of a given level of unemployment can be reduced. We are currently training about 1.5 million people per year at a cost of $1.5 billion. Some would urge that 1.5 million is not a large fraction of a labor force of 80 million.

A contradictory theory, and one that was adopted by the Nixon Administration, is that inflation can be cured only by a sharp increase in unemployment to above 4 percent. According to this theory, wages can be kept down by having a pool of unemployed, and prices will be restrained by lessening total spending.

The debate about the level of unemployment was resolved. Unemployment in 1970 was almost 6 percent of the labor force. It seems unlikely that in the next year or so we can repeat the rapid poverty reduction of the 1965–69 years via erosion of unemployment, at least by conventional fiscal and monetary expansionism. This conclusion has led some to advocate extraordinary measures aimed specifically at employment of the poor. One such measure is to pay employers a subsidy or grant them a tax credit aimed at covering the costs of recruiting, training, and upgrading disadvantaged workers. The idea is to induce employers to hire from the back of the line, so to speak. This may merely spread the cost of a given level of unemployment among workers in a different way, or it may lead to a reduction in the overall level of unemployment. Subsidy measures of this type are difficult to administer and uncertain as to outcome. But we are giving it a try now with the Jobs in the Business Sector program, under which the government is contracting to pay an average subsidy to run for one year of $2800 per disadvantaged recruit to cooperating employers, who have pledged to fill 500,000 new permanent jobs in this way. (Some employers are cooperating with the program but prefer not to sign a contract and take a subsidy.) An alternative would be to allow any employer who hired a certified hard-core unemployed person and retrained him for a stated period to claim a tax credit for some fraction of wages paid. A variation on this idea is to pay all employers a subsidy to induce them to hire low-productivity workers on a permanent basis. The subsidy would be greater, the lower the wage rate. It would thus be a kind of negative payroll tax and would induce the employer to substitute low-skill labor for high-skill labor.

A still different proposal is to expand public and nonprofit employment of unskilled and inexperienced workers. The extreme form of this is for the federal government to become the "employer of last resort," i.e., to stand ready to put any and all persons who want but cannot find a job on the government payroll at the minimum wage. A more moderate proposal is to fund out of tax revenues, by means of matching grants to state and local governments and nonprofit organizations like hospitals, a limited number of jobs. These selected employers would agree to expand their employment at prevailing wages by hiring through standard channels. Hopefully, this would be less inflationary than a generalized expansion of employment, although we must note that it would tend to force wages up at the low end and hence have some cost-raising effects.

The direct approach of using public funds to create jobs for poor people is popular among people across the polical spectrum. It accords with the Puritan ethic and the high value we put upon work. The cost of providing a million jobs by some combination of the methods described above would be about $4 billion a year, assuming that employers will take on added workers without a subsidy for added fixed plant and equipment costs. The amount of poverty reduction and narrowing of the poverty-income gap which would be accomplished thereby would depend on who got the jobs. If the jobs were genuinely new jobs and did not merely shift the financial responsiblity for jobs that would have existed anyway, and if all the job-takers were from poor families who would otherwise have had no wage income, then several million people could be taken out of poverty and the poverty-income gap could be cut by $4 billion, less administrative and supervisory costs. The taxpayers would lose $4 billion, but the nation would gain the value of whatever the extra employees produced. However, it is likely that there would be a certain amount of slippage in practice. Not all the jobs will be jobs that would not have been open otherwise, and not all the takers will be from poor families. If, as seems likely, there were more than 1 million people who would like to have such jobs, it would raise difficult questions of how to ration the jobs. It would be likely to produce the inequitable situation of some poor persons getting paid less for working at private jobs than others are paid for equivalent public jobs.

Job subsidy for the poor is a troubling route,[9] but one that is worth at least a cautious trial.

---

[9]It is more troubling than a carefully designed negative income tax of the kind described below. The latter is, as Henry Simons said of the income tax, a device which involves "no fundamental disturbance of the whole system" (cited supra, chap. 2, p. 26). For that reason one might expect conservatives to favor it more than they do job subsidy. However, it does not appear that they do.

2. Cash Transfers

Another approach to the poverty problem is that of cash transfers.[10] The transfer system described in Part B was paying out public cash benefits totaling $43 billion in 1967. These benefits reduced the number of persons in poverty by about 20 million, and cut the poverty-income gap from $25 billion to $10 billion. Could we not expand the set of money transfers to reduce that remaining gap to zero? The answer is that we could, but there is no plan which will take everybody out of poverty for an amount equal to the poverty-income gap, which is now about $10 billion. A negative income tax with a guarantee at the poverty line and a 50 percent tax rate (hence a break-even point at twice the poverty line) would have cost at least $25 billion in 1967 in benefits and income tax forgiveness over and above what we were then spending on transfers. These net benefits would go to some 80 million people, leaving the upper 120 million to pay the $25 billion on top of the taxes they are now paying. Worry about subjecting working people to a 50 percent marginal tax rate—and note that we are talking not about a few categorical poor, but about 40 percent of the population—leads some to advocate lowering the offset tax rate to, say, 33⅓ percent, thereby raising the break-even points to three times the poverty lines and placing the whole tax load, which would then be expanded to cover about $50 billion of net new

---

[10]For a comparison of alternatives, see Christopher Green and Robert J. Lampman, "Schemes for Transferring Income to the Poor," *Industrial Relations* 6 (February 1967), 121–37 (Reprint No. 10, Institute for Research on Poverty, University of Wisconsin, 1967). Also see Robert J. Lampman, "Transfer Approaches to Distribution Policy," *American Economic Review* 55 (May 1970), 270–79 (Reprint No. 61, Institute for Research on Poverty, University of Wisconsin, 1971).

Some readers will find it of interest that the following discussion is quite at odds with the views of Eveline M. Burns. Professor Burns offers the intriguing insight that social welfare measures are evolutionary in character and that we have moved from a public assistance stage to a social insurance stage and are now witnessing the transformation of social insurance (which is the victim of its own success) into something quite different, namely a system concerned more with adequacy than with equity. This stage, she believes, will be followed by a shift to assurance of a minimum income for all, ultimately via a guaranteed minimum income plan, but in the near future by the adoption of free health services, a flat old-age pension (with social insurance as a double-deck aid to the middle class and private pensions as a top deck for the upper class), and a flat children's allowance. She sees an income-conditioned benefit of the negative income tax variety as a retrogressive move on her evolutionary ladder, one which would move us back to the preinsurance stage of separating the poor from the nonpoor ("Social Security in Evolution: Towards What?" *Proceedings* of the Industrial Relations Research Association, 1964).

transfers to the lower two-thirds of the population, on the upper one-third. That amount would require a near doubling of the money now being transferred by all public and private sources. In any event, what may look at the outset like an easy problem takes on greater scope as one surveys the alternatives. Certainly it is a major disservice to rational discourse to suggest, as many have done, that the United States could eliminate poverty if we were only willing to transfer an additional $10 billion to the poor. There is no way to get that $10 billion into the hands of the poor without spending far more than that.

There are, however, numerous ways to fill part of the poverty-income gap. One way is to expand social insurance. One-third of all poor persons are in households where the head does not work. Most of these heads are aged, disabled, or are women with small children in the home. Many, but not all, of these nonworking heads are already receiving either assistance or social insurance or veterans' benefits or some combination of them. It has been estimated by Secretary Wilbur Cohen that raising the general level of Social Security benefits by 50 percent and doubling the minimum benefit (now $60 a month for a retired worker) would take 4.4 million people out of poverty. This would cost about $11 billion, the greater part of which would go to nonpoor beneficiaries or beneficiaries made nonpoor by receipt of the greater benefits. More narrowing of the poverty-income gap per dollar of transfer would follow a raising of public assistance payments in the low-income states. This could be done by having the federal government play a stronger role, perhaps an exclusive role, in setting standards for and administering categorical assistance. Total cash benefits under public assistance amount to about $7 billion. Adding one or two billion dollars to this total by increasing benefits in such low-income regions as the South, where almost half the nation's poor are found, would seem to be a high-priority use of antipoverty funds.

One cannot go very far in considering transfer payments as a way to narrow the poverty-income gap without confronting two overlapping issues: what to do about children in intact families and what to do about "the working poor." About half the poor are children under 18, and the greater part of these are in families headed by a man who works all or most of the time. Few of the latter group are either on assistance or eligible for it. To extend assistance to cover able-bodied men with jobs seem inappropriate because of the disincentives to work which are entailed. These disincentives to work are of two kinds. One arises out of the guarantee or lump-sum benefit which is assured if the family has no other income. If this is high enough to approach the poverty line it may induce some to quit work altogether. The other disincentive is associated with the amount by which the benefit is reduced as earnings rise. This is a "tax rate," in effect, and in public assistance it has traditionally been as severe as 100 percent, or a dollar-for-dollar reduction in benefit for every dollar earned.

To avoid these disincentives to the poor but to put some added cash in their hands, many have argued that we should adopt a children's or family allowance as sixty-two other nations have done. This would have the added advantage of treating all families alike and with none of the stigma of public assistance. But such an allowance scheme has an enormous price tag attached to it. There are about 70 million children in the nation. To pay each of them $25 per month would involve a gross outlay of $21 billion per year. However, it would be reasonable to accompany the allowance with a withdrawal of income tax exemptions for children, which would recover $6 billion of revenue. If in addition the allowance itself were taxable, another $3 billion would be recovered at existing income tax rates, some of it from the poor, since all income over the parents' exemptions would now be taxable. This leaves $12 billion to be paid for by higher tax rates. If the poor are going to benefit from the allowance less the tax, it follows that some nonpoor are going to have to pay an added tax in excess of the allowance. The higher the "break-even" level of income is set, the fewer the taxpayers to bear the net cost of the plan and the greater the addition to already high marginal tax rates which they must bear. Also, the higher the break-even level, the more the child allowance payments net of tax go to nonpoor families. In all such schemes, only a fraction of the gross outlay is a net addition to the incomes of the poor. For example, in the plan just outlined, a $21 billion outlay would achieve about $3.5 billion additional income for the poor. It would, of course, do nothing for unrelated individuals and couples without children. Thus, while a children's allowance would not adversely affect the work incentives of the poor, it does have certain disadvantages.

One way to avoid these disadvantages, without at the same time falling back into the difficulties of public assistance, is to adopt a variation of the negative income tax which I call an "income supplement for the working poor." The typical working-poor family has an income of about $2500, so for them the size of the guarantee in the event of no earnings is not the critical thing. Lady Rhys-Williams said that the "lion in the path" of an adequate guarantee was a not unreasonable unwillingness of society to pay an amount that invited able-bodied men to retire from the work force. Her solution was to have a work test as a qualification for benefits. The alternative here proposed is, by contrast, "all carrot and no stick." Much more critical than the level of the guarantee is the matter of what the supplement is at their ordinary earnings level and what the marginal tax rate is on added earnings. So an income supplement for a new category called the working poor could sensibly have a low guarantee and a low set of tax rates.[11]

The key features of such an income supplement for the working poor are reflected in a schedule of allowances for a family of four persons (Table 9.2). Parallel tables would be established for unrelated individuals

Table 9.2.   Net Allowances for Four-Person Families under Income Supplement for the Working Poor

Income before allowance	Net allowance	Income after allowance	Marginal tax rate
$ 0	$750	$ 750	—
500	750	1250	$ 0
1000	750	1750	0
1500	750	2250	0
2000	750	2750	0
2500	500	3000	50
3000	250	3250	50
3500	0	3500	50

and for each family size. It would dramatize the unique purpose of the income supplement to deny people the right to receive the supplement at the same time as they receive public assistance.

This income supplement would accomplish the main purpose of a family allowance but would confine its benefits to the poor. It would reduce, but not eliminate, the sizeable incentive some poor families have to separate in order to claim AFDC benefits. It would pay benefits not only to families with children but to all others who are poor and not on assistance. It would cost about $4 billion (in contrast to the $21 billion gross cost of the family allowance described above) to get $4 billion of net benefits into the hands of the poor (which compares favorably with the $3.5 billion in the case of the family allowance). Hopefully, this amount would fall each year as the number of working poor dwindled

---

[11]The extreme formulation of this idea would be to have a zero guarantee and below zero (or negative) marginal tax rates. One way to implement this extreme is a wage supplement payable directly to the employee. Suppose a worker earning $1.00 per hour were to receive a supplement of 50 cents for every hour worked. This would encourage him to do more work. However, this would be extraordinarily difficult to administer and would tend to pay benefits to many nonpoor families. I tend to reject this idea, but see it as one worth further research. A second way to implement this idea is to match total earnings rather than hourly wages up to a level of (say) $1500, and then tax added earnings at 50 percent. This would confine benefits to poor families.

due to economic growth. It would also fall as we succeeded in reducing unemployment and nonparticipation in the labor force by active labor market policy or by the subsidy programs to create new jobs for the poor.

President Nixon's Family Assistance Plan, which he proposed in August 1969, is an interesting combination of the ideas reviewed above. The several provisions of the legislation would (1) raise the minimum benefits for the so-called adult categories via Old Age Assistance, Aid to the Blind, and Aid to the Permanently and Totally Disabled; (2) abolish Aid to Families with Dependent Children as a federally assisted categorical program; and (3) institute a new federal plan of negative income tax-type benefits for all families with children—this plan would have a guarantee of $1600 for a family of four, a zero tax rate on the first $720 of earnings, and a 50 percent tax rate on added earnings up to a break-even income level of $3920. The proposed legislation would also (4) condition these benefits by a family resources or assets test, and by a work test; (5) require states to continue benefits in the form of supplements to those in the broken-family category to the extent their state guarantees are now above the new federal guarantee of $1600; and (6) require the states to administer these supplementary benefits in conformity with all the conditions and key definitions which govern the new federal benefit.

The net result of the Nixon proposal would be to add about $3 billion to the amount of cash transfers going to the poor. It would add about 14 million more persons to the welfare rolls. It would narrow the difference in treatment of equally poor families in the several states, and similarly, it would narrow the difference between families headed by men and those headed by women.

The Family Assistance Plan has been under scrutiny in Congress, where the following broad issues are being weighed: how much to transfer, how to divide transfers between cash and in kind, how much emphasis on children, how intensely to concentrate on poverty reduction, how high a marginal tax rate, what existing transfers should be reduced to help finance any new benefit. But, even after those issues are resolved, there are numerous, somewhat more technical issues to be settled. A simple family allowance plan does not have to contend with some of these issues, but other plans do. Some of these are: (1) Should the plan have a work test associated with it, as does FAP? Should the work test apply to all adults? Should the penalty for failing to work less than full time be severe? (2) Should the income subject to the special offset tax be defined broadly (as in FAP) or narrowly? Should Social Security benefits be included, and hence taxed? (In FAP they are taxed at 100 percent.) Should work expenses and child care expenses be deductible?

(3) Should the family be defined so as to leave a choice as to what persons, and hence whose incomes, are to be included in calculating a family's benefits? (4) What income period should be used in determining benefits? Most negative income tax analysts have assumed one year would be the period, but public assistance administrators use one month. (5) How should a new benefit be articulated with existing public assistance programs? Should AFDC-U be dropped? Should a new plan set maximum combined tax rates for those families simultaneously on FAP and a state benefit program? (6) How should the new cash benefit be related to in-kind benefits such as food stamps and Medicaid? If food stamps are priced inversely to income they take on the basic characteristic of a negative tax and hence have a marginal tax rate associated with them. That marginal tax rate could combine with other tax rates to raise the overall tax rate on some families to very high levels. Should the food-stamp bonus be calculated after the FAP benefit, but before the state supplementary payment, or after both? Or should all food stamps be dropped and the funds be diverted to financing the more generous negative income tax? (7) How should the plan be administered and by whom? Should it be handled by the states or by the federal government? If the latter, should it be done by the Internal Revenue Service, the Social Security Administration, or a new agency?

Those seven questions indicate the complexity of introducing a new type of income-conditioned benefit into the existing system of transfers.

3. The Role of Services

In addition to cash benefits, federal, state, and local governments transfer goods and services, principally educational and health services, worth over $65 billion. Of these, the poor receive an estimated $25 billion worth. The services referred to cover a wide range. In addition to education and training, there are health-service programs like Medicaid and Medicare; housing services, including public housing and rent supplements; direct provision of food; and legal aid and social casework services. In addition to public provision of such services, private groups like churches, associations of professional and business leaders and the poor themselves have undertaken to help the poor. Since 1964 significant efforts have been made to equalize access to general community services. The police, the courts, the schools, welfare administrators, churches, libraries, hospitals, family planning clinics, county agents, home economists, employment service directors, and many others have learned that there is much they can do to improve the quality of service to the poorest and least demanding of their clients. Tax experts have turned our attention to ways in which the tax system could be made less regressive. This learning process has been led by a new crop of specialists in the several professions on the problems of the poor. In many cases they have learned to work with previously unidentified leaders of the poor. They have established new rights for the poor, new ways to enforce old rights, and have spread knowledge of such rights among the people. There can be no doubt that this campaign to equalize community services has improved the prospects for some poor persons to seize opportunities to escape from poverty.

Some poor persons need not just equal treatment but remedial or compensatory programs to overcome deficiencies of historic origin. If a child from a poor background is to be ready for school, he may need Head Start training, health care, and even food. Some specialists are stating that equal educational achievement will be possible in slum schools only if we spend considerably more per child in those schools than we do in suburban schools. Some youngsters need a way to finance completion of high school or vocational training. The Neighborhood Youth Corps and Job Corps point the way. If we are to assure real equality of opportunity for higher education, those from poor families need the outreaching services of an Upward Bound program and special scholarship help. We have learned that some of those compensatory programs do assist many youngsters to achieve more in school than they otherwise might. And it is reasonable to expect that they will contribute over a long span of time to poverty reduction.[12]

Another special technique of the war on poverty has been to seek what the Economic Opportunity Act called "maximum feasible participation" of the residents of poverty areas in what is known as "community action." This is aimed at involving the poor in community improvement, bringing their ideas and interests into planning and administering antipoverty efforts, and getting them to feel a part of the community in which they live. Community action projects have been diverse in character. Some have concentrated on recreation, some on housing or health care, or legal services, or Head Start, or job training. It is hard to evaluate all these efforts by so many different agencies, but there are some outstanding examples of efficient performance in response to the felt needs of poor people. Some of them have pioneered in new ways of delivering services, which are being adopted nation-wide by established agencies. There is much controversy about the future of community

---

[12]Ribich's valuable study of *Education and Poverty* urges caution in relying on compensatory education as a weapon against poverty.

action.[13] Participation by an organized poor community (remembering the poor are now only 11 percent of the population) may be a necessary condition in some localities of successful prosecution of the poverty war. It is not, however, in any locality a *sufficient* condition for rapid progress against income poverty. The aim is not to organize poverty but to eliminate it, and that can be done only by programs and policies of substance, and not by technique alone.

Budget limitations force public and private agencies to make hard choices among worthwhile cash transfers and services for the poor. These choices call up considerations of both equity and efficiency. Equity would require that we treat all people in like circumstances equally. This argues for a few broad programs rather than a large number of localized ones. Efficiency considerations point to getting more income to the poor through jobs and cash transfers rather than to a set of specialized noncash transfers like rent supplements and food subsidies. This will allow individual choice by poor people in selecting what they most want and need for self-improvement.

Earlier in this book we noted our special concern with what we identified as "income poverty." That concern "builds in" a bias for cash income as opposed to in-kind transfers. But there are other reasons for favoring cash benefits, as ways to reduce income poverty. (Please note that in-kind transfers may be amply justified as means toward other significant goals.) One of these has to do with the disincentives and inequities that arise with certain patterns of in-kind transfers to the poor. Consider the case of health care.[14] Suppose free health care is offered to the poor and that this offer is the equivalent of a health insurance policy that would cost $500 per year. This means that by earning the extra dollars that would take them over the poverty line, a family would lose the $500 worth of insurance protection. This "notch" could be modified by compelling the poor to pay part of the $500 premium. However, at a near-poor income level, that family would be unlikely voluntarily to spend $500 on private health insurance. This would suggest that perhaps the only fair way to get adequate medical care to the poor is via a system of nationwide health insurance or socialized medicine

---

[13]For a critical view, see Daniel P. Moynihan, *Maximum Feasible Misunderstanding: Community Action in the War on Poverty* (New York: Free Press, 1969). For a favorable view, see Levine, *The Poor Ye Need Not Have with You.*

[14]This case illustrates the conflict between two "mentalities" we identified above (pp. 148, 149) as the "minimum provision mentality" and the "horizontal and vertical equity mentality."

open to rich and poor alike. Another argument against noncash benefits has to do with their effectiveness in getting people out of income poverty. Many critics assign a low priority to health expenditure because it appears to have a low payoff in terms of getting people out of poverty.[15] Some noncash programs take a long time to bear fruit in terms of income, e.g., preschool training.

SUMMARY

Thinking along these lines leads me to certain conclusions about how to allocate funds in the early 1970s, assuming the goal is to accelerate the reduction of income poverty, and assuming that antipoverty funds are limited. I would give highest priority to cash help for the poorest of the poor by allocating $2 billion to raising public assistance minimums in the low-income states. I would assign second priority to an income supplement for the working poor with a first-year outlay of $4 billion. Neither of these programs would take anybody out of poverty but, combined, they would cut the poverty-income gap from $10 billion to $4 billion. Then, as a third priority, I would allocate $4 billion to increasing job-related education and training and to creating jobs for the poor. I would expect this to reduce the number of persons in poverty by 2 million and to interact with the income supplement in reducing the poverty-income gap.

Those are simply the reflective conclusions of one observer. They are based on a particular point of view concerning the goal of reducing income poverty. They are also based on the assumption that there will be steady improvement in the quality of many generally available services and in the dignity accorded to the poor. These qualitative matters, and many nonexpenditure items, such as willingness to enforce laws important to the well-being of the poor, cannot be reflected in budget allocations.

In evaluating the above priorities, or any other set of priorities, it is important to see them in the perspective of what we are already spending in antipoverty efforts. In 1967 the American system of transfers was operating on a scale of $132 billion. Of this total the pretransfer poor received cash and service transfers of about $50 billion. In return they

---

[15]See Myron J. Lefcowitz, "Poverty and Health" (Discussion Paper No. 71, Institute for Research on Poverty, University of Wisconsin, 1970). I have the same understanding with respect to expenditures on housing (see Larry L. Orr, "The Welfare Economics of Housing for the Poor" [Discussion Paper No. 33, Institute for Research on Poverty, University of Wisconsin, 1967]).

paid about $10 billion in the form of contributions and taxes. Hence they were net beneficiaries of about $40 billion. This is one measure of the scale of our continuing war on poverty.

Underlying the future success of these expenditures, and of the new ones proposed, which total $10 billion, is successful management of the economy to keep the average unemployment rate from rising any higher. If the long-range forces of economic growth continue to favor us, we can expect them to reduce poverty at a rate of 1.5 million or so persons per year in addition to the one-shot gains referred to above. Further one-time gains would follow from reduction of unemployment. It is hard to be very precise about this, but it is possible that this combination of programs and policies could reduce the number in poverty to under 13 million persons and cut the poverty-income gap to under $3 billion by 1974, thereby setting the stage for the complete elimination of income poverty by 1976. That year, when we will celebrate the two hundredth anniversary of the Declaration of Independence, would be an appropriate one to achieve that goal.

In saying that the income-poverty problem can be solved in the near future, i.e., within this decade, we are not saying that all the causes and symptoms associated with that problem are going to disappear. Even after we eliminate income poverty, there will still be gross inequality of wealth and income; some will still be dependent upon others; no doubt there will be ugly discrimination on account of color; much housing, health care, and education will be less than ideal; not all the near-poor will be full participants in society; not all slums and depressed areas will be transformed into model communities. Income poverty, as presently defined, can be removed from the scene without resolving all these other social questions, but doing away with it may contribute to improvement on all these questions. Ending income poverty does not require and will not achieve a transformation of society. It is a modest goal. Income poverty is only part of the broader problem of poverty. And poverty, as we noted in Part A, is a subtopic of the general issue of inequality. We should proceed, not with utopian expectations, but with the belief that achievement of this particular goal, along with progress toward other social and economic goals, will be a worthy achievement in the slow evolution of the good society. Dedication to the goal of eliminating income poverty requires that we scrutinize every expenditure made in the name of the poor to make sure that a great share of the benefits go to them. Dedication to other goals requires that we be alert to the possibility that the side effects and costs of such expenditure may, in some cases, be unreasonably high. Ending income poverty is not, of course, the only social goal we have for our nation, and it is important that in striving to achieve that goal we contribute at the same time to a broader range of purposes that will make an America in which all citizens have incomes above the poverty level a better place in which to live.

BACKGROUND WRITINGS BY THE AUTHOR

The following published and unpublished works by the author are reflected to some degree in this book.

"Income, Ability, and Size of Family" (with D. A. Worcester, Jr.). *Journal of Political Economy,* October 1950.

"The Significance of Personal Income Distribution Data." Western Economic Association *Proceedings,* September 1953.

"Income Distribution and Economic Welfare." *Current Economic Comment,* May 1954.

"Recent Changes in Income Inequality Reconsidered." *American Economic Review,* June 1954.

"Making Utility Predictions Verifiable." *Southern Economic Journal,* January 1956.

"The Effectiveness of Some Institutions in Changing the Distribution of Income." *American Economic Review,* May 1957.

"Recent Thought on Egalitarianism." *Quarterly Journal of Economics,* May 1957.

"Paying the Price of Higher Fertility." *Problems of U.S. Economic Development,* Vol. II, Committee for Economic Development, 1958.

"Taxation and the Size Distribution of Income." *Tax Revision Compendium,* Vol. III, U.S. House of Representatives, Ways and Means Committee. Washington, D.C.: Government Printing Office, 1959.

The Low Income Population and Economic Growth. Study Paper No. 12, U.S. Congress, Joint Economic Committee. Washington, D.C.: Government Printing Office, 1959.

The Share of Top Wealth-holders in National Wealth, 1922–1956. Princeton, N.J.: Princeton University Press for the National Bureau of Economic Research, 1962.

"Income and Welfare: A Review Article." *Review of Economics and Statistics,* September 1963.

Editor's Introduction to *Social Security Perspectives,* by Edwin E. Witte. Madison: University of Wisconsin Press, 1963.

"People's Capitalism: Myth or Promise." *New Republic,* 1963.

"Goals for the American Economy." In *Farm Goals in Conflict.* Iowa State University, Center for Agricultural and Economic Development, 1963.

"How Fast Can We Reduce Poverty?" *Challenge,* March 1964.

"Prognosis for Poverty." *Proceedings* of National Tax Association, 1965.

"Negative Rates Income Taxation." Unpublished paper for the Office of Economic Opportunity, 1965.

"Approaches to the Reduction of Poverty." *American Economic Review,* May 1965.

"Income Distribution and Poverty." In *Poverty in America,* edited by Margaret Gordon. San Francisco: Chandler Publishing Company, 1965.

"The Anti-Poverty Program in Historical Perspective." *The Nation,* 7 June 1965.

"How Much Does the American System of Transfers Benefit the Poor?" In *Economic Progress and Social Welfare,* edited by Leonard H. Goodman. New York: Columbia University Press, 1966.

"Ends and Means in the War on Poverty." In *Poverty Amidst Affluence,* edited by Leo Fishman. New Haven, Conn.: Yale University Press, 1966.

"Population Growth and Poverty Reduction." In ibid.

"Toward an Economics of Health, Education, and Welfare." *The Journal of Human Resources,* 1966.

"Income Distribution of American Labor." In *The Vista of American Labor,* edited by William Haber. Voice of America Forum Lectures, 1966.

"Schemes for Transferring Income to the Poor" (with Christopher Green). *Industrial Relations,* February 1967.

"Adding Guaranteed Income to the American System of Transfers." *Social Action, 1967.*

"Recent U.S. Economic Growth and the Gain in Human Welfare." In *Perspectives on Economic Growth,* edited by Walter W. Heller. New York: Random House, 1968.

"Distribution of Wealth." In *International Encyclopedia of Social Sciences,* 1968.

"Negative Income Taxation: A Challenge to Social Engineers." *Virginia Law Weekly* and *Dicta,* University of Virginia Law School, 1968.

"Expanding the American System of Transfers To Do More for the Poor," U.S. Congress, Joint Economic Committee, 1968 (revised version in *Wisconsin Law Review,* 1969).

"What We Have Learned about Poverty," *The Nation,* 9 December 1968.

"Transfer and Redistribution as Social Process." In *Social Security in International Perspective,* edited by Shirley Jenkins. New York: Columbia University Press, 1969. (Also available as Reprint No. 49, Institute for Research on Poverty, University of Wisconsin, 1970.)

"Steps To Remove Poverty from America." Unpublished paper presented to the Wisconsin Symposium, 1969.

"Transfer Approaches to Distribution Policy," *American Economic Review,* May 1970. (Also available as Reprint No. 61, Institute for Research on Poverty, University of Wisconsin, 1970.)

"Nixon's Family Assistance Plan," Discussion Paper No. 57, Institute for Research on Poverty, University of Wisconsin, 1969. Reprinted in part in *Readings in Economics,* edited by Paul A. Samuelson. New York: McGraw-Hill, 1970.

"Economic Policy Objectives and Problem Areas." In *Social Economics for the 1970's,* edited by George F. Rohrlich. New York: Dunellen Publishing Company, 1970.

"Public and Private Transfers as Social Process." In *Redistribution to the Rich and the Poor,* edited by Kenneth Boulding and Martin Pfaff. Belmont, Calif.: Wadsworth Publishing Co., forthcoming.

INDEX